THE RESOURCES
OF THE
BRITISH EMPIRE

BY LORD BEAVERBROOK

LANE PUBLICATIONS

23 ST. BRIDE STREET, E.C.4

1934

Made and Printed in Great Britain by
Hazell, Watson & Viney Ltd. London and Aylesbury

CONTENTS

ACKNOWLEDGMENT

A great part of the statistics published in this book have been derived, by permission, from *Whitaker's Almanack* for 1934, to the publishers of which my thanks are due.

Official publications, such as the Board of Trade Returns, the Statistical Abstract of the British Empire, publications of the Colonial Office and of the Colonial Governments, have also been consulted for additional material.

EMPIRE FREE TRADE

The British Empire is the greatest association of free peoples in the world. It occupies a quarter of the land surface of the globe. Its population is a quarter of the total number of human beings in the world. The production of its fields, its seas, its factories, and its workshops is immense and varied beyond imagining. Its potential wealth has no limit. It is at once the most wonderful expression of the genius of a race and the finest example of fruitful co-operation between diverse peoples.

Empire Free Trade is the only dynamic policy for the British Empire to-day. It has a meaning, a message, and a constructive programme to offer to every unit in that huge assembly of states and territories.

It is firmly based on two main principles:

1. The peoples of the Empire can support themselves in comfort and prosperity from the abundant resources of their own soil and the work of their own hands.

2. An incalculable prosperity lies within their grasp if they devote themselves to developing their Imperial heritage, but this can only be done if the competing products of foreigners are excluded.

Freed from the menace of competition from countries with lower standards of life, rejoicing in the free interchange of the goods of one unit of the Empire with those of another, the British peoples can insulate themselves from the economic follies and miseries of the rest of the world.

They have led mankind in the achievement of

liberty for all. Now they can provide an example to the world of plenty wisely husbanded and widely shared, and of a security in strength which none dares challenge.

The method which is proposed to carry the policy into effect is the simple, well-tried device of duties imposed upon imports from foreign countries.

This tariff system prevails in the colonies of foreign Powers. Unlike schemes for Government regulation and restriction of trade by means of quotas and other Socialistic inventions, it allows commerce and industry the utmost liberty to develop in their own way.

There is no mystery about the policy of Empire Free Trade. It means what its name implies: The achievement of the greatest possible measure of Free Trade between the constituent parts of the Empire.

This is the ideal which those of us who believe in the cause keep firmly before us. But we do not shut our eyes to any of the facts. The Dominions have complete self-government. They have already taken steps to protect their secondary industries by high tariffs against foreign goods and by lower tariffs against articles coming from the United Kingdom.

These are facts which we accept. And we certainly do not presume to ask the Dominions to make sacrifices for which they are not ready.

In the case of the Crown Colonies, a decision by the Parliament at Westminster can, without delay, bring into being a full measure of Empire Free Trade applied to the whole of the Colonial Empire.

The immediate task of the Empire Free Trade movement has therefore been stated thus:

1. The creation, now and here, of a Customs Union for Great Britain and the Crown Colonies, so that there may be a flow of trade between

each of these colonies, and between any of them
and the ports of the United Kingdom as free and
as untrammelled as between, say, Lancashire and
London.

2. The completion of the tariff barrier against
foreign goods entering Great Britain. This will
be done by imposing duties against foreign
meats and by raising to an adequate protective
level the existing tariffs on such commodities
as eggs and manufactured dairy products.

3. An approach, carried out as swiftly as possible and as near as circumstances will allow,
towards the ideal of Empire Free Trade with
the Dominions also.

If there are difficulties here, they have been
created by half a century of neglect of the
Imperial opportunity. But these difficulties can
be overcome by British Governments.

The Empire Free Trade movement exacts resolute patience as well as unremitting energy from
its supporters. And we can count with confidence
on the fact that our brothers in the Dominions
have their eyes fixed on the same goal as we have.

Meanwhile, the practical formula evolved by the
Empire movement will ensure us a real advance
along the path we wish to tread:

First place to the home producer in his own
market.
Second place to other Empire producers.
Third place to the foreigner.

The policy, with its bold lines and its broad
Imperial vision, is one that appeals to every man
who has faith in the destinies of the British race,
and who has lost patience with politicians who
stand between the race and its glorious future.

But it also attracts the business man, who sees
the British Empire as a great producing and

trading concern in a state of woeful disorganization.

Empire Free Trade involves a cleaning up of the economic structure—an application of sound business common sense to the trading of the Empire. It is a splendid vision taking shape in concrete, feasible form.

The time has long passed by when we can allow trade to develop in an anarchic and self-destructive manner. It is ridiculous, for example, that we should buy the greater part of Egypt's cotton crop while Egypt buys her cotton piece-goods from Japan.

The Empire Free Trade policy in action would not tolerate such a preposterous situation!

If Egypt will not buy the cotton manufactures of Lancashire, we must develop the production of raw cotton in the Sudan and other Empire territories. And in any case, this is a development of Empire resources which should be carried out without delay.

By doing so we should create in the cotton plantations we founded a rich new market for our manufactures.

There is no reason why we should import any of our raw materials, with the exception of petroleum and a few commodities of small importance. But if we are to supply the needs of our factories, we must set to work to cultivate our Empire garden in a purposeful, orderly manner.

The case for Empire Free Trade does not depend upon ingenious pleading. It is founded upon the facts of Imperial trade which are to be found in official publications and standard works of reference. It needs no other argument.

The outstanding facts are stated in a concise form in the pages that follow. They constitute the main outlines of Empire knowledge such as should be known to every man and woman in the country, however slight his or her interest in politics.   They are an anatomy of the Empire.

They tell their own story of Imperial wealth and Imperial opportunity, of the difficulties we have to face in moving forward to the goal of Empire Free Trade, and of the follies of the past which we must strive to wipe out.   A brief study of these figures will, it is hoped, enable a man to make a persuasive speech in public on the Empire theme or to conduct a convincing argument with his friends.

But the book will only have served its purpose if it enlarges and enriches the vision of Empire which every Briton has in less or greater degree.

I

GREAT BRITAIN

It is not necessary to do more than give a few items of statistical information of the simplest character in relation to Great Britain.

The area of Great Britain and Northern Ireland is 93,984 square miles. The population is 46,047,046. There are 19,343 miles of railways.

The developed resources of Britain are visible in her industrial areas. But the undeveloped resources are more easily overlooked, and it is to these that the attention of the Empire Free Trade movement turns. For it is an integral part of the Empire scheme to bring about the greatest possible development of these neglected resources of Britain.

Unhappily, there has been a one-sided development of resources in the country for generations past. Manufacturing industry has undergone immense expansion, while agriculture has languished and fallen into decay.

The net value of the industrial production of Britain in 1930 was estimated at £1,433 millions, while the figure for the agricultural production of the country was £235 millions (1925 figures).

Until recently, the public turned a deaf ear to the farming industry, but fortunately a change in attitude has come about. It began with the Empire Crusade in 1929. An important element in that campaign was the forceful and picturesque presentation of the case for developing agriculture.

The Empire Crusaders made full use of their opportunities, finally convincing the public that the agricultural production of the country could be considerably increased, provided that duties were imposed on foreign imports of foodstuffs.

This remarkable change in the nation's point of view was accompanied by great political disturbances in the Conservative Party. The leaders of the party resolutely turned their faces against the taxes on foreign food or indeed against any impediment in the way of the free import of those foodstuffs. They alleged that it was impossible to win a general election if the unpopular cry '' Stomach Tax '' was attached to the Conservative Party.

Mr. Stanley Baldwin himself told the writer in picturesque terms that he could not consent to any tax on foodstuffs. If he allowed himself to be dragged into such a position, he would be like the man who set out with a beautiful, clean white waistcoat and patted a passing St. Bernard dog, only to find the prints of the dog's muddy paws indelibly marking his waistcoat.

By the summer of 1931 the Conservative Party had accepted the policy. In the general election in the autumn of that year, the policy did more than any other factor to carry the day for the National Government, with the exception perhaps of the propaganda so successfully directed by Lord Snowden.

Unhappily, while the principles of the Empire policy have been conceded by the Government, the practice has been delayed. In consequence, there has been no increase in agricultural production in the last three years.

When the policy is put into effect, not only to sustain prices, but to increase production, the most splendid results will follow. Britain is the only country in the world with under-developed agricultural resources and with a market at its own door capable of absorbing its entire production.

At the present time that market is supplied by foreign countries, especially by the Argentine and

Denmark. The total British imports of foodstuffs amounts to £350 millions a year, and of this no less than £200 millions is taken from foreign countries.

As for the Argentine and Denmark, these two foreign countries depend absolutely on the British market. They depend for their livelihood on the sales of their foodstuffs to us. But they do not spend their money on British manufactures. Denmark buys largely in Germany and the Argentine in the United States.

If we give to our own farmers the market at present enjoyed in Britain by these foreigners, we could give employment to thousands of men and women who now go idle. But we should do more than that. We should create in the rural districts a vast new home market spending hundreds of millions of pounds a year. That market would be protected by tariffs against the competition of foreigners. It would be reserved to the British industrial worker.

Agriculture, though the chief, is not, of course, the only neglected resource of Britain. There are also coal and shipping. With these I should like to deal, but it is not possible within the limits set by a book of this nature.

DOMINIONS

Commonwealth of Australia

Australia is a continent with a contiguous island, Tasmania, lying between the Indian and Pacific Oceans.

Area just under 3 million square miles. Population in 1933, 6,623,754; yearly increase now slightly under 100,000.

The *Commonwealth* has existed only since January 1st, 1901, and was formed by the union of six States, independent of each other, but each forming a part of the British Empire.

States.	Area.	Population.
New South Wales . .	309,432	2,600,428
Victoria	87,884	1,818,050
Queensland	670,500	945,565
South Australia . . .	380,070	580,849
West Australia . . .	975,920	438,113
Tasmania	26,215	227,473

These are the six States which united to form the Commonwealth. A large part of the territory of South Australia, with an area of 520,000 square miles and a population of only 4,300, is now administered as " Northern Territory " by the Commonwealth Government.

The population is almost entirely European and mainly British. There are about 60,000 aborigines, 21,000 Chinese, and 3,000 Japanese.

The estimated value of the output of Australian agriculture and industry in 1931–2 was £305 millions. The principal crop is wheat, of which 190 million bushels were produced in 1931–2.

Pastoral industry is more important, Australia having about 112 million sheep, and a wool crop of over 1,000 million lb. of wool in the grease, about one-fourth of the Empire's production. The value of all the minerals produced in 1931 was nearly £13½ millions.

Manufacturing output in 1931-2 was valued at £106,456,000. There were 21,657 industrial establishments, employing 336,658 workers.

The exports of Australian domestic merchandise were valued at £74,176,000 in 1931 (rather less than half their value in 1925). The chief items are: butter, £6·9 millions; flour, £3 millions; wheat, £12·5 millions; beef and mutton, £3·7 millions; wool, £27 millions. In addition, she exported gold and silver to the value of £12·8 millions, nearly all of it as gold coin.

In 1931, exports to U.K. were £33 millions; to Empire, £7 millions; to foreign countries, £34 millions. The fall from the 1925 high level was about equally distributed among these three sources, each being reduced by about half.

The imports of Australia in 1931 were valued at £60,560,699, thus distributed: from U.K., £23,276,000; from Empire, £8,500,000; from foreign countries, £27 millions. The principal items were: machinery, about £5 millions; apparel and attire, just over £1 million; metals and metal manufactures, tools and cutlery, about £3 millions; cotton goods, £3,600,000; motor chassis, £722,000.

Latest Figures.—1931 was a year of depression. The figures for the last six months of 1933 (the first half of the trade year 1933-4) are very much better. Exports of merchandise, £49,406,000; imports, £28,853,000. Taking gold and silver into account, Australia had in those six months a *favourable balance* (exports over imports) of £24 millions.

The Australian Tariff.—Australia, being a dominion, has absolutely independent powers of making her own tariff (just like the United Kingdom, in fact).

The tariff arrangements between Australia and the U.K. are regulated by the agreement signed at Ottawa in August 1932. The chief points are:

1. Free entry *for three years certain* of Australian eggs, butter, poultry, and cheese—position to be reviewed at end of that period.

2. Empire producers to have free entry for certain agricultural products, while similar foreign produce is to be subject to duty (not yet carried out).

3. A margin of preference of 2*s*. a gallon on wine.

4. Australia to give tariff protection " only to those industries which are reasonably assured of sound opportunities for success " (Article of Agreement). Australian duties to be based on the principle that United Kingdom producers shall have " full opportunity of reasonable competition on the basis of the relative cost of economical and efficient production " (Article 10).

Australia is a *Federal* Commonwealth within the British Empire. The original six States still have their own Governments and Legislatures, and can make laws on the subjects *not handed over to the Federal Government*, but in case of inconsistency, Federal law is superior. The present Governor-General (Sir Isaac Isaacs) was selected by the Federal Government (first time of doing it). The Senate consists of 6 members from each State; the House of Representatives of 75 members, the number from each State being in proportion to population, with a minimum of 5.

In 1931, a plan (" the Premiers' Plan ") for restoring the national finances (both Commonwealth and State) was adopted. It is being carried out with great success.

Railways, 27,799 miles; 157,260 miles of telegraph wires. A Beam Wireless Station was opened in 1927.

Defence.—Australia has a fleet of 4 cruisers, 1 sloop, 5 destroyers, and some auxiliaries. The Navy consists of 339 officers and 2,783 men. The Australian Army, of about 28,000 men, is voluntarily recruited. The Air Force consists of 48 officers and 261 airmen.

During the Great War Australia sent 329,682 troops abroad, of whom 58,961 were killed. She incurred a war expenditure of £288 millions.

Papua

A part of New Guinea, placed under the authority of the Commonwealth of Australia in 1906. Area, 90,540 square miles. Population, 275,000 natives and 1,128 whites. Capital, Port Moresby.

Trade in 1932–3: Imports, £218,300. Exports, £248,712.

Territory of New Guinea

A part of the former German colony of New Guinea, placed under Australian mandate. Area, 93,300 square miles. Population, 390,000 natives and 2,900 whites.

Trade in 1931–2: Imports, £779,397. Exports, £1,108,619.

The Dominion of Canada

The dominion comprises all land in America north of U.S.A. except Newfoundland, Greenland (to Denmark), and Alaska (to U.S.A.).

Area, 3,684,463 square miles, of which 226,979 are freshwater lakes. Population, 1931, 10,376,786

(375,000 more males than females). Population
has doubled since 1901.

Racial origins numerous, but just over half the
population is British, rest mostly European. The
population of French descent numbers rather less
than 3 millions. France took possession of the
country in 1534. Wolfe conquered Quebec, 1759.
Canada became British, 1763. In 1867, Ontario,
Quebec, Nova Scotia, and New Brunswick were
united in the Dominion of Canada. Other States
joined later.

Province.	Area (sq. m.).	Population (1931).
Alberta	255,285	731,605
British Columbia	355,855	694,263
Manitoba	246,512	700,139
New Brunswick	27,985	408,219
Nova Scotia	21,068	512,846
Ontario	412,582	3,431,683
Prince Edward Island	2,184	88,038
Quebec	594,534	2,874,255
Saskatchewan	251,700	921,785
Yukon	207,076	4,230
North-West Territories	1,309,682	9,723

The population of Quebec is mainly French by
origin and language and Roman Catholic by
religion. The river St. Lawrence, the Great Lakes,
and the Trans-Continental railways cross the
dominion from side to side (Canadian Pacific
Railway completed 1885), and the country is built
on them as on a backbone.

The natural resources of Canada are magni-
ficent. Its soil is particularly suited to cereals.
In 1932, the acreage under wheat was 27·2 millions
and the crop 429 million bushels; oats, 13·1 million
acres and 392 million bushels; barley, 3·75 million
acres and 81 million bushels. The finest wheat in
the world is Canadian, and it sets the standard
for quality and price of all others. The fodder
crops are also very large, e.g. hay and clover, 8·8
million acres, yielding $13\frac{1}{2}$ million tons.

In dairy produce the output in 1932 was:

creamery butter, 214 million lb.; dairy butter, 107 million lb.; cheese, 120 million lb.

Fur farming and fisheries are also important natural resources.

Lumbering is a very great Canadian industry. Its output in 1931 was valued at about £40 millions.

The mineral output of Canada in 1932 was valued at £36,500,000. The chief items were: gold, £12,600,000; copper, £3 millions; nickel, £1,400,000; coal, £7,400,000.

The manufactures of Canada are important (especially in relation to her population and her comparative " youth " as a country). In 1931, industrial establishments had a capital of about £1,000 millions, with a gross output valued at £540 millions; employees numbered 557,428, and the total pay roll was £125 millions. The average weekly wage per employee was therefore between £4 and £4 5s.

Canada is neighboured by the United States, and the boundary is often merely an artificial line. Canada uses the same money (dollars and cents) as the United States, and large amounts of American capital are sunk in Canadian industries. These facts affect to a marked extent the economic position and policy of the dominion.

The foreign trade of Canada is very extensive, because the productive natural resources are far greater than the consuming power of her population.

Exports of domestic produce in 1932 were valued at £117,627,046, to which gold and silver, worth £10,092,000, must be added. The chief items were (in millions of £): wheat, 23·8; wheat flour, 3·9; barley, 2; nickel, 2·5; printing paper, 21·2; wood pulp, 4·8; wood and timber, 8·0; cheese, 2·2; fish, 4·7; apples, 1·3; furs, 2·5.

Her principal customers were (in millions of £): United Kingdom, 35·7; Empire, 8·9; United States, 48·2; other foreign countries, 24·7.

Imports in 1932 were valued at £118,807,753, the principal items being (in millions of £) : iron and steel and manufactures thereof, 8·5; machinery, 7·2; coal, 7·3; cotton yarn and piece-goods, 2·1; chemicals, 4·8; petroleum, 7·8; whisky, 3·2; woollen fabrics, 2·4.

The chief sources of her imports were (in millions of £) : United Kingdom, 21·8; Empire, 8·5; United States, 72·2; other foreign countries, 16·2.

In common with the rest of the world, Canada's foreign trade has fallen off severely during the " slump." In 1929, her imports were £260 millions and her exports £278·6 millions.

Customers for Canada's chief exports 1931 (in millions of £, small items omitted) :

	U.K.	Empire.	U.S.A.	Other Foreign Countries.	Total.
Grain products . . .	16.9	2.3	0.8	13.0	33.0
Butter, cheese, eggs .	2.4	—	—	—	2.7
Ores	2.2	—	5.4	—	8.3
Motor-cars and parts .	—	1.4	—	1.2	2.7
Wood, timber and manufactures . .	1.4	—	11.4	1.8	15.1
Newsprint . . .	1.0	0.1	19.4	0.8	22.3

Suppliers of Canada's Chief Imports, 1931 :

	U.K.	Empire.	U.S.A.	Other Foreign Countries.	Total.
Sugar . . .	—	3.9	—	—	4.2
Alcoholic beverages .	4.6	—	—	0.8	5.5
Coal . . .	1.0	—	6.5	—	7.5
Iron and steel bars, rods, plates . .	1.3	—	3.3	—	4.9
Iron and steel manufactures . .	0.8	—	4.2	—	5.3
Electrical machinery and apparatus .	0.4	—	3.3	—	3.7
Other machinery .	0.7	—	5.8	—	6.6
Motor-cars and parts .	—	—	5.5	—	5.5

The tariff-making body in Canada is the Dominion Parliament, acting (as in the United Kingdom) on proposals made to it by the Dominion Government. Canada was the first self-governing Colony (as it then was) to grant, in 1897, a preference to the United Kingdom of one-fourth of any then existing duty.

The United Kingdom-Canadian Agreement made at Ottawa, in 1932, provides, among other things, that protection against United Kingdom products shall only be given to Canadian industries reasonably assured of success, that Canadian protective duties shall not exceed a level which will give United Kingdom producers " full opportunities of reasonable competition on a basis of economical and efficient production," and that a Tariff Board should be established to advise the Canadian Government.

During the Great War 13·5 per cent. of the male population, or a total of 530,000, served overseas, and 6 per cent. suffered casualties.

The cost of the war to the dominion was approximately $2,000 millions.

The Dominion of New Zealand

Area and Population.—The Dominion of New Zealand is distant about 1,200 miles south-east of the mainland of Australia, and consists of three main islands in the South Pacific Ocean, known as the North, South, and Stewart Islands, with several groups of smaller islands lying at some distance from the principal group.

By Proclamation, issued September 10th, 1907, the style and designation of the Colony of New Zealand was altered to the Dominion of New Zealand. The dominion has an area of 105,155 square miles, and a population (excluding Maoris) in 1933 of 1,465,833, the yearly increase averaging 15,000 persons.

The population is composed mainly of Europeans, numbering at the 1926 Census 1,338,167. There were also 63,600 Maoris, 3,374 Chinese, and 2,928 of other races.

Production.—New Zealand is a pastoral rather than an agricultural country, but grows a sufficient quantity of wheat and oats for her own requirements. The principal types of livestock numbered in 1933:

Sheep	27,755,000
Cattle (including dairy cows) .	4,182,000
Pigs	586,000

During the year ended June 1933, the dominion produced 288 million lb. of wool, 2,439,000 cwt. of butter, 1,781,000 cwt. of cheese, and 9,853,000 lamb and 4,356,000 mutton carcases were slaughtered for meat production.

Coal is the main source of mineral production, with output valued at £1,842,000 in 1932. Gold is also of value. Production totalled £1,019,000 in 1932.

In the fiscal year 1931–2 there were 4,969 factories in New Zealand having a total output of £67,813,000 and employing 68,697 persons.

Import and Export Trade.—For the year ended June 1933 exports were recorded in New Zealand currency at £37,470,000 (sterling equivalent, £31,516,000). The principal items of export in 1932 were:

	£
Butter valued at	10,639,000
Frozen meat	8,436,000
Wool	5,742,000
Cheese	4,951,000
Gold	1,092,000
Hides and skins	1,074,000

In the same year exports to the United Kingdom amounted to £32,449,000; to other Empire countries, £2 millions; and to foreign countries, £2,512,000.

The proportion of New Zealand's exports sent to the United Kingdom has risen from 73·6 per cent. in 1929 to 87·7 per cent. in 1932.

Total imports into New Zealand for the year ended June 1933 were recorded as £22,191,000 (New Zealand currency equivalent £25,290,000).

The principal items of import in 1932 were:

	£
Iron and steel manufactures . .	1,825,000
Electrical apparatus and machinery .	959,000
Other machinery	796,000
Motor-cars and parts	1,294,000
Cotton piece-goods	1,372,000
Other textiles	4,000,000
Petroleum	1,845,000

In 1932, imports from the following countries were valued at:

	£
The United Kingdom . . .	11,496,000
Australia	2,691,000
Canada	1,007,000
United States	3,267,000
Japan	434,000

British countries accounted for 71·8 per cent. of the total and foreign countries for 28·2 per cent. The share of the United Kingdom in New Zealand's import trade has risen slightly from 46·2 per cent. in 1929 to 49·9 per cent. in 1932.

Customs Tariff.—In the United Kingdom-New Zealand Agreement, signed at Ottawa in August 1932, the main proposals affecting the tariff arrangements between the two countries were:

(1) For three years, eggs, poultry, butter, cheese, and other milk products of New Zealand origin will enter free into the United Kingdom, while on such goods of foreign origin a duty will be levied.

(2) In order to give a preference on goods of New Zealand origin, a duty will be levied by the United Kingdom on the following goods entered from foreign countries: apples, pears, and honey.

(3) Article 10: " His Majesty's Government in New Zealand undertake that no reduction shall be made in the margins of preference now enjoyed by United Kingdom goods over those of any foreign country."

Before the Ottawa Agreement New Zealand had already granted United Kingdom goods a high margin of preference which, on most commodities, was from 20 per cent. to 25 per cent. *ad valorem.*

Government.—Parliament consists of a General Legislative Council appointed by the Governor, at present consisting of 21 members, appointments being made for seven years, and a House of Representatives consisting of 80 members elected for three years. Four of the members are Maoris elected by the natives.

For purposes of local government the dominion, like the British Isles, is divided into counties and ridings, with incorporated boroughs, under elected county and municipal councils, town, road, electric power, and harbour boards.

In March 1933 there were 3,315 miles of Government railway lines in use and 168 miles of private lines. There were also 12,415 miles of telegraph lines, with 64,221 miles of wire.

Defence.—The New Zealand Defence Force consists of the Permanent Force, the Territorial Force, the Air Force, and the Senior Cadets.

The New Zealand Permanent Force comprises 80 professional officers, and the strength of the (volunteer) Territorial Force is 955 officers and 8,138 other ranks.

The New Zealand Division of the Royal Navy comprises 2 cruisers, 1 depot ship, 1 trawler, and 1 oil-tanker.

New Zealand sent 100,000 men for service overseas in the war; of these, 17,000 were killed. The dominion raised £82 millions in war loans.

Western Samoa

A group of Pacific islands, formerly in the possession of Germany, is under the mandate of New Zealand. Area, 1,133 square miles. Population, 40,229. The chief products of the islands are copra, cocoa, bananas, and rubber.

Trade in 1932: Imports, £150,900. Exports, £183,028.

Newfoundland

A large island on the north-east side of the Gulf of St. Lawrence. The oldest British colony, formally occupied in 1583.

Newfoundland administers the Labrador coast.

In normal times government is carried on by a Governor, Executive Council, and two Houses of Legislature. In November 1933 a Royal Commission, under the chairmanship of Lord Amulree, reported that the administration of the dominion should be taken over by the Governor and 6 Commissioners, 3 appointed by the United Kingdom Government and 3 by Newfoundland. This was later put into effect. The British Government guaranteed the Newfoundland Government loans, and proposed to make grants to stabilise its finances. It was estimated these grants would not exceed £2 millions.

Area, 42,750 square miles. Labrador, 120,000 square miles. Population, 286,345. Capital, St. John's.

The coast of Newfoundland is rugged and mountainous, but the interior contains fertile valleys, with a climate favourable to agriculture, and a great wealth of forests of spruce, fir, pine, and birch.

The population is chiefly found in the coastal
regions, nearly 10,000 being engaged in fishing—
cod in summer and seal in winter. Agriculture,
mining, and lumbering are carried on, and large
pulp and paper mills have been established. The
chief exports are codfish, cod and seal oil, pulp
and paper, and herrings. The total value of the
fishery products in 1931–2 was $6·4 millions.

Labrador forms the most easterly portion of
the North American continent and has
valuable fisheries. The inhabitants are mainly
Eskimos.

Trade of Newfoundland in 1931–2: Imports,
$18,135,651, of which $3 millions from Britain,
$8 millions from Canada, and $5·7 millions from
the United States. Exports, $26,689,476, of which
$7·9 millions to Britain, $1·3 to Canada, and $10
millions to the United States.

At the Ottawa Conference, Britain agreed to
impose duties on foreign imports of cod-liver oil
and chilled and frozen salmon, while Newfoundland gave 10 per cent. preference margin on a
large number of British articles, as well as preferences to some kinds of produce from the Crown
colonies.

During the war, Newfoundland contributed
12,000 men to the fighting forces of the Empire, as
well as 3,000 who enlisted in Canadian and other
forces.

The cost of the war to Newfoundland is estimated
at $15 millions.

The Union of South Africa

Area and Population.—The provinces of the
Union extend from the southernmost point of the
African Continent to the course of the Limpopo
River, and include all the British territories
within those limits, with the exception of Basutoland and the Swaziland and Bechuanaland Protectorates.

The Union of South Africa was constituted under the South Africa Act, 1909, which united the self-governing colonies of the Cape of Good Hope, Natal, the Transvaal, and the Orange River Colony.

The area of the Union is 472,347 square miles, and the estimated population in 1932 was 8,250,900, of which 1,859,000 were estimated to be European and 6,391,000 non-European.

Province.	Area in sq. miles.	Estimated population in 1932, European.
Cape of Good Hope . .	276,966	758,000
Natal	35,284	181,300
Transvaal . . .	110,450	714,100
Orange Free State . .	49,647	206,000

At the 1921 Census, the non-European population was composed of 4,697,000 Bantu peoples, 165,600 Asiatic peoples, and 545,500 persons of mixed and other races.

South-West Africa is administered under mandate as an integral part of the Union of South Africa. Its estimated area is 317,725 square miles, and the population in 1932 was approximately 275,900, of whom about 32,000 were Europeans.

Production.—The principal crops and quantities produced in the Union (including all native production) in 1930 were as follows: wheat, 637 million lb.; barley, 105 million lb.; oats, 301 million lb.; and maize, 4,477 million lb. The pastoral industry is very important, the Union possessing (including all natives) in 1930 10½ million cattle, 48 million sheep, and nearly 1 million pigs.

Gold-mining continues to be the chief source of the Union's mineral wealth, the value of the output of gold in 1932 being £49,766,000. Diamonds were produced to the value of £1,679,000; coal, £2,733,000, and copper, £254,000.

There were 7,730 factories in the Union in 1929–30, employing a total of 218,585 people (all races included), and the gross value of output amounted to £112 millions. The principal manufacturing industries are foods, textiles, and printing and publishing works.

Import and Export Trade.—Total exports from the Union of South Africa amounted to £68,938,000 in 1932, compared with £97,757,000 in 1929. The principal items of export in 1932 were: gold, £47½ millions; wool, £6½ millions; diamonds, £2 millions; fruit, £2 millions; and hides and skins, £¾ million.

In 1933, out of a total value of exports of £67,651,000, exports to the United Kingdom amounted to £55 millions; to other Empire countries £1,632,000, and to foreign countries, £10,979,000.

The United Kingdom's share of the total exports from the Union has risen from 64 per cent. in 1929 to 81 per cent. in 1933.

Total imports into the Union were £32,790,000 in 1932, compared with £83,450,000 in 1929. The principal items imported in 1932 were: machinery, £2,473,000; food and drinks, £2,413,000; cotton textiles, £2,382,000; clothing, £1,202,000; woollen manufactures, £986,000; hardware, £1,533,000; electrical machinery, £1,521,000, and iron and steel (including agricultural implements), £1,272,000.

In 1933, out of the total imports into the Union of £46,449,000, the United Kingdom supplied £23,707,000; other British countries, £3,482,000; foreign countries, £19,259,000, which includes a total of £6 millions from U.S.A., £3 millions from Germany, and £2 millions from Japan.

The share of the United Kingdom in the total import trade of the Union has risen from 43 per cent. in 1929 to 51 per cent. in 1933.

Customs Tariffs.—The United Kingdom-Union of South Africa Agreement, signed at Ottawa in

August 1932, contained the following important points regarding customs tariffs arrangements between the two countries:

(1) For a period of three years at least, eggs, poultry, butter, cheese, and other milk products will enter the United Kingdom free of duty if of South African origin, while on such goods entering from foreign countries a customs duty will be imposed.

(2) In order to grant a preference on goods of South African origin, the United Kingdom will impose duties on the following goods entering from foreign countries: oranges, grape-fruit, peaches, plums, grapes, apples, pears, dried fruits, canned fruits, maize, and copper.

(3) A margin of preference of 2s. a gallon on wine will be granted by the United Kingdom.

(4) By a series of tariff amendments the Union of South Africa Government propose to increase the margin of preference granted to goods of United Kingdom origin.

Government.—The legislative power of the Union is vested in the King, represented by the Governor-General, a Senate, and a House of Assembly. The Senate consists of 40 members. Eight are nominated by the Governor-General-in-Council, and 32 are elected, 8 for each Province. The House of Assembly consists of 150 elected members. Members of both Houses must be British subjects of European descent.

A Provincial Council in each Province has power to legislate by ordinance on certain subjects specified in the South Africa Act (1909), and on such other subjects as may be delegated to it. All ordinances passed by a Provincial Council are subjected to the veto of the Governor-General-in-Council. Members of the Provincial Council are elected on the same system as Members of Parliament, but the restriction as to European descent does not apply.

The total open mileage of Government-owned railway lines in March 1933 was 13,100 miles. During 1933, 39,445 miles of telegraph wires were in use, and 452,450 miles of telephone wires.

The Union sent 221,500 soldiers to fight in the war, including 28,000 coloured recruits. There were 19,000 killed.

The cost of the war to South Africa was £33 millions.

The Irish Free State

Consists of the 26 Southern Irish counties, and is by the constitution a co-equal member of the British Commonwealth of Nations. The Legislature (Oireachtas) consists of the King and two Houses, the Chamber of Deputies (Dail Eireann) and the Senate (Seanad Eireann).

Area, 17,024,481 acres. Population, 2,971,992, of whom 2,751,269 are Roman Catholics.

The armed forces amount to 546 officers and 5,350 men.

The Irish Free State is predominantly agricultural. In 1932 there were 760,306 acres under corn crops, 656,374 under roots and green crops, and 2,281,747 under hay. The principal products were: oats, 627,200 tons; potatoes, 3,015,418 tons; turnips, 3,383,962 tons; mangolds, 1,637,500 tons, and hay, 4,743,147 tons. Livestock: 4,025,080 cattle, 3,460,816 sheep, 1,108,315 pigs, 149,048 goats, 446,064 horses.

In the fisheries 1,200 were employed, the total value of all fish landed being £227,074.

Trade in 1932: Imports, £42,574,222, of which £28,869,206 from Great Britain, and £3,759,270 from Northern Ireland. Exports, £28,940,228, of which £22,846,814 to Great Britain and £3,104,479 to Northern Ireland.

INDIA

The Indian Empire

Area and Population.—The Indian Empire extends over a territory larger than the continent of Europe without Russia. Legally, " British India " means all territories governed by the King-Emperor through the Governor-General of India, or through any governor or other officer subordinate to the Governor-General of India.

The total area of India proper is about 1,809,000 square miles, with a population of nearly 353 millions (about three-fourths of the population of the British Empire). The British Provinces, as distinguished from the Indian States, comprise 61 per cent. of the area and nearly 77 per cent. of the population.

Owing to the operation of the caste system, India is broken up into a large number of mutually exclusive aggregates, the members of which are forbidden by an inexorable social law to marry outside the group to which they themselves belong. A caste may be defined as a collection of families, or groups of families, bearing a common name, which usually denotes, or is associated with, a specific occupation. The chief castes and races are (Census 1931) :

Brahman	.	.	.	.	15,207,000
Chamar	.	.	.	.	12,195,000
Ahar, etc.	.	.	.	.	14,170,000
Rajput	.	.	.	.	10,743,000
Burmese	.	.	.	.	8,596,000
Jat	.	.	.	.	8,377,000
Maratha	.	.	.	.	6,113,000

The population by religions in 1931 includes:

Hindus	239,000,000
Mohammedans	77,700,000
Buddhists	13,000,000
Christians	6,000,000
Sikhs	4,300,000
Jains	1,200,000
Parsis	109,000

Over 66 per cent. of the population was in 1931 dependent on agricultural and pastoral pursuits.

Production.—Agriculture is by far the most important occupation of the people of India. Of the total area of 229 million acres sown in 1931–2, approximately 10 per cent. was under wheat; 35 per cent. was under rice; 43 per cent. was under food-grains and pulses; 7 per cent. was under oilseeds; 8 per cent. was under cotton, jute, and other important crops.

The total area under irrigation was 52 million acres.

The output of coal in India in 1930 was 23,803,000 tons; of crude petroleum, 311 million gallons; of salt, 1,711,000 tons; of manganese ore, 839,000 tons, and of gold, 329,000 oz.

In India the ancient village handicrafts still survive. Cotton-weaving is by far the most important hand industry. There were 8,148 factories in 1930 employing 1,528,000 persons. These included: 310 cotton mills, which produced 867 million lb. of yarn (mostly of low counts) and 590 million lb. of woven goods; 100 jute mills, which contained 1,224,000 spindles and 61,834 looms; 17 woollen mills; 11 paper mills, and 11 breweries.

Import and Export Trade.—Total exports from India in 1932–3 (sea-borne trade) were valued at £155,069,000. This figure is only about three-fifths of the 1928–9 value of exports. India's principal exports in 1932–3 were:

                                              £ millions.
          Raw jute and jute manufactures   .   23½
          Raw cotton   15
          Tea   .   .   .   .   nearly   13
          Rice   11
          Seeds 8½
          Leather and metals   .   .   .   each   3½

The United Kingdom's share of total exports in 1932–3 was 28½ per cent.; that of other British Empire countries, 17½ per cent.; of Japan, 10½ per cent., and of other foreign countries, 43½ per cent.

Imports into India in the same year totalled £103,505,000, a figure which was slightly less than half that of 1928–9. In 1932–3 the principal items imported were:

                                              £ millions.
          Cotton goods   17
          Raw cotton and cotton yarn .   .   8
          Machinery   8
          Iron and steel 3.3
          Brass and other metals .   .   .   4
          Mineral oils   5
          Silk goods 2½
          Sugar   3
          Motor-cars and woollen goods
                                   each nearly   2

In 1932–3 the United Kingdom supplied 36·8 per cent. of India's import trade; other Empire countries, 8 per cent.; Japan, 15½ per cent., and other foreign countries, 39·7 per cent.

Customs Tariffs.—With certain exceptions, the general rate of duty on imports into India is 25 per cent. *ad valorem.* On certain items a preference is granted on goods of United Kingdom origin; for example, on cotton, twist, yarn or thread, the duty is 25 per cent. *ad valorem* if of British manufacture and on goods of other countries 50 per cent. *ad valorem*; and on plain grey cotton piece-goods the *ad valorem* duties are the same.

Under the United Kingdom-India Agreement signed at Ottawa in August 1932, the principal points affecting customs tariffs were:

(1) The United Kingdom undertook to grant a preference on the following goods of Indian origin by levying a duty on similar foreign goods: wheat, rice, a number of vegetable oils, and linseed; also coffee.

(2) The United Kingdom undertook to " co-operate in any practical scheme for promoting the greater use of Indian cotton in the United Kingdom."

(3) India undertook to grant a margin of preference of 10 per cent. *ad valorem* to a wide range of goods of United Kingdom origin.

Government.—The Secretary of State for India is the head of the Indian Administration in England, and as a member of the Cabinet he is solely responsible to, and represents the supreme authority of, Parliament. Indian Government business in England is transacted at the India Office and at the Office of the High Commissioner for India. Subject to the Secretary of State's direction, the supreme executive authority in India, in both civil and military affairs, is the Governor-General-in-Council. The Governor-General's Executive Council now contains 7 members as well as himself.

In accordance with the Government of India Act, 1919, the Indian Legislature consists of the Governor-General, and two Chambers, viz. the Council of State and the Legislative Assembly. Although the Government does not command a majority in the Indian Legislature, it is necessarily given the power to reject adverse votes, since its responsibility is not to the Indian Legislature, but to Parliament.

British India is divided into sixteen local Governments and Administrations, ten of which are under Governors, and six are under Chief Commissioners who are under the immediate authority of the Governor-General.

Under the Government of India Act, 1919, the Local Governments are given a large measure of independence of the Supreme Government. The Supreme Government is given authority over certain subjects classified as " central," such as defence, political relations, railways, tariffs, etc., while other administrative heads, such as education, public works and sanitary services, excise, justice, etc., are wholly or partly handed over to Provincial Governments. The Provincial Legislative Councils have an elected majority. The Governor has powers of veto in regard to proposed legislation affecting the safety or tranquillity of his Province.

The Indian Constitution is in process of change, and after three Round Table Conferences and a number of Commissions, His Majesty's Government have set out their proposals for constitutional reform in a White Paper. These proposals provide for a federal system of government, with self-government at the centre and in the Provinces. A Joint Select Committee of both Houses of Parliament has been set up to report on them in consultation with Indian representatives.

There are 42,813 miles of railways open for traffic in India, and 532,283 miles of telegraph wires in use.

Defence.—The sanctioned strength of the Army in India is:

British troops and officers	68,900
Indian troops and officers	155,300
Indian Army Reserve	40,000
Auxiliary Force	36,000
Indian States Force	44,700
Indian Territorial Force	19,000

During the Great War, 1,381,000 officers and

men were sent on service overseas for India. The total Indian casualties were 36,696. The money effort of India in the war amounted to £132 millions.

The Indian fleet consists of four sloops, two patrol boats, one survey ship, and various auxiliary craft.

Aden, on the southern coast of Arabia, is an important coaling station. It is constituted as a province under the control of the Indian Government. Area, 75 square miles. Population, 51,478.

Aden is a free port, with a total sea-borne trade in 1931 of £6,984,600.

IV

CROWN COLONIES IN AFRICA

Basutoland

A native territory in South Africa administered by a High Commissioner, who is the Governor-General of the Union of South Africa.

It lies between the Orange Free State, Natal, and Cape Colony.

Area, 11,716 square miles. Population, 498,971, of whom 1,603 are Europeans. Capital, Maseru.

Basutoland has an excellent climate, and is one of the finest grain-growing areas in South Africa.

The Basuto rear vast herds of cattle, sheep, and goats. The chief exports are wool and mohair.

Trade in 1931: Imports, £462,733, of which £15,152 from United Kingdom. Exports, £251,427.

For Customs purposes Basutoland is dealt with as part of the Union of South Africa.

Bechuanaland

A native protectorate of South Africa administered by a Governor-General, who is the High Commissioner for the Union of South Africa.

Area, 275,000 square miles. Population, 152,983, of whom 1,743 are Europeans. The headquarters of the administration are at Mafeking, Cape Province.

A pastoral country, although Kaffir corn, mealies, etc., are grown and reaped when rainfall is adequate. Cattle, 426,000. The railway from

Kimberley to Mafeking traverses the protectorate.

In 1932, Bechuanaland imported £572,000 from the United Kingdom and exported £80 to it.

For customs purposes Bechuanaland is dealt with as part of the Union of South Africa.

British Cameroons

A mandated territory on the east boundary of Nigeria and administered as part of that colony.

Formerly part of the German colony of Kamerun, which was divided between Britain and France in 1919, and in 1922 placed under mandate by the League of Nations.

Area, 34,599 square miles. Population, 781,611. Chief ports, Victoria and Tiko.

The surface of the territory is remarkably varied. There are coastal swamps, dense forests, and high grasslands. The natives breed cattle and produce guinea corn.

Trade in 1932: Imports, £103,462, of which £31,559 (30 per cent.) from Great Britain. Exports, £158,294, of which £10,974 (7 per cent.) to Great Britain.

Under the terms of the mandate, no tariff preferences are given to British goods.

Gambia

A colony in West Africa, occupying the lower basin of the Gambia River. Recognized as British in 1783 and created a separate colony in 1843.

Area, 4,132 square miles. Population, 199,520. Capital, Bathurst.

The chief export is ground-nuts, 95 per cent. of the total export. Over half of the export is sent to France.

Trade in 1932: Imports, £292,700, of which £149,323 (50 per cent.) from Great Britain. Exports, £406,894, of which £84,043 (21 per cent.) to Great Britain.

Gambia buys from Britain nearly twice as much as she sells to Britain.

Gambia gives tariff preference to a limited number of British goods. In some cases, where the general rate is 12½ per cent., the preferential rate is 10 per cent. In others, such as cotton-piece goods, where the general rate is 20 per cent., the preferential rate is 15 per cent.

Gold Coast

A Crown colony in West Africa, between the French colonies of the Ivory Coast and Dahomey. It consists of four parts, the Gold Coast colony, Ashanti, the Northern Territories, and Togoland.

There have been British settlements on the Gold Coast since 1651. The Crown colony was created in 1874. Ashanti was annexed in 1901, when the Northern Territories were also placed under British protection. Togoland is a portion of an ex-German colony administered under mandate.

The colony is administered by a Governor, aided by a nominated Executive Council. There is also a Legislative Council for the Crown colony, with an official majority.

Area, 91,843 square miles. Population, 3,268,307 natives and 3,146 non-natives. Capital, Accra.

The principal products are cocoa, gold, manganese, and diamonds. Cocoa accounts for about 70 per cent. of the total exports. The colony has great forest wealth, largely untapped. Railways, 952 miles.

Trade in 1932: Imports, £5,605,219, of which £3,273,593 (60 per cent.) from Great Britain. Exports, £7,892,905, of which £3,431,199 (43 per cent.) to Great Britain.

The Gold Coast is subject to the operation of the Anglo-French Convention, which forbids it to give preferential tariff treatment to British imports against imports from France or other countries with which Britain has commercial treaties containing " most-favoured-nation " clauses.

The Gold Coast, with Nigeria and Jamaica, provides us with the best opportunity for the expansion of British trade in the Crown colonies.

Kenya

A colony and protectorate in East Africa, acquired by cession and conquest between 1888 and 1918. Official majority in the Legislature.

Area, 224,960 square miles. Population, 3,076,343, of whom 17,249 are Europeans and 34,966 are Indians.

Capital, Nairobi. Mombasa, the chief port, has the finest harbour on the East Coast of Africa.

Great areas of the colony consist of pasture lands, but there are also extensive districts suitable for agricultural development.

Coffee, cotton, maize, and sisal are grown. Railways, 1,627 miles.

Kenya and Uganda are one unit for Customs purposes. Trade in 1932 (Kenya and Uganda): Imports, £4,862,859, from the United Kingdom £1,915,347 (40 per cent.). Exports (Kenya), £2,280,982, of which £1,771,559 (77 per cent.) to the United Kingdom.

Kenya and Uganda are included in the area of the Congo Basin Treaty, and so cannot give Customs preference to British imports.

Nigeria

A colony and protectorate in West Africa acquired by treaty-cession in 1891.

Area (including the mandated territory of the Cameroons), 372,674 square miles. Population, 19,928,171. Capital, Lagos.

Administered by a Governor and a nominated Legislative Council.

The staple articles of production are palm oil and kernels, ground-nuts, cocoa, and tin. There are extensive coalfields and immense quantities of valuable timber in the forests. Railways, 3,048 miles.

Trade in 1932: Imports, £7,243,143, of which £5,358,891 (74 per cent.) from Great Britain. Exports, £9,628,944, of which £3,504,895 (36 per cent.) to Great Britain.

Nigeria buys from Britain nearly £2 millions more than she sells.

Cotton goods accounted for £2,559,788 of the imports. The principal export items were: palm kernels, £2,695,964; palm oil, £1,514,310; cocoa, £1,461,451; ground-nuts, £1,873,831, and tin ore, £549,283.

Nigeria, under the Anglo-French Convention, cannot give better tariff treatment to British imports than to those of France or of other countries with which Britain has " most-favoured-nation " treaties.

Nigeria, with the Gold Coast and Jamaica, furnishes the best opportunity for the expansion of British trade in the Crown colonies.

Nyasaland

A protectorate in East Africa to the west and south of Lake Nyasa.

Area, 37,596 square miles. Population, 1,609,915, including 1,901 Europeans. Proclaimed a protectorate in 1891. Principal towns, Blantyre, Limbe, and Zomba.

Considerable cultivation of tobacco, in which there is an export trade, and also of tea, cotton, and fibre. Railways, 348 miles. Roads, 3,142 miles.

Trade in 1932: Imports, £740,385, of which £410,152 (55 per cent.) from Great Britain. Exports, £788,998, of which £651,099 (82 per cent.) to Great Britain.

Britain buys substantially more from Nyasaland than she sells to her.

Nyasaland is included in the area in which, under the Congo Basin Treaty, no tariff preference to British goods is allowed.

Rhodesia, Northern

A Crown colony in Africa to the north of the Zambesi.

Area, 288,400 square miles. Population, 1,393,258, of whom 10,553 are Europeans. There is a Legislative Council with a majority of official members. Capital, Livingstone.

There are vast areas of land suitable for arable farming and grazing. Over 2½ million acres are under settlement by white farmers. Maize is the chief crop, but tobacco and coffee are also grown. Stock-raising is important. Cattle, 477,000. There are extensive mineral deposits, the copper mines being destined to supply a great proportion of the world's needs.

Trade in 1932: Imports, £1,965,000; from Great Britain, £597,000 (30 per cent.); from British Empire, including United Kingdom, £1,394,400. Exports, £2,436,000; to United Kingdom, £777,777 (32 per cent.); to British Empire £838,868.

Part of Northern Rhodesia is included in the area to which the Congo Basin Treaty applies, and is therefore not able to give preference to British goods.

Rhodesia, Southern

A self-governing colony in southern Africa, lying between the Zambesi River and the Transvaal.

Area, 150,344 square miles. Population, 1,200,000, of whom 52,000 are Europeans.

Responsible government was instituted in 1923. The colony is administered by a Governor, with an Executive responsible to the Legislative Assembly. Capital, Salisbury.

The colony has valuable mineral deposits. The gold output in 1932 was valued at £3,366,000. There is also a considerable production of silver, copper, coal, diamonds, lead, chrome, iron, platinum, and other metals. The staple crop is maize. Other products are tobacco, cotton, and citrus fruits.

The cultivated area is 432,000 acres, more than half of it under maize. Cattle, 2,747,000. Railways, 1,360 miles. Road motor services cover 1,505 miles.

Southern Rhodesia is suitable for settlement by Europeans, and has immense possibilities of development in agriculture and cattle-raising.

Trade in 1932: Imports, £4,272,127, of which £1,873,112 (43 per cent.) from Great Britain. Exports, £5,387,251, of which £3,328,324 (61 per cent.) to Great Britain.

Southern Rhodesia gives substantial tariff preferences to British imports over a wide range of articles.

Typical rates:

Piece goods: General rate 20 per cent., British rate 10 per cent. Clothing: General rate 20 per cent., British rate 12 per cent. Iron and steel manufactures: General rate 5 per cent., British rate 3 per cent.

Sierra Leone

A Crown colony in West Africa, ceded to Britain by treaty 1787.

Area, 28,000 square miles. Population, 1,770,000. There is a Legislative Council, partly elected and partly nominated. Capital, Freetown.

The colony has considerable tropical forest wealth, its chief products being palm kernels, kola nuts, palm oil, and ginger. Railways, 310 miles.

Trade in 1932: Imports, £1,248,346, of which £822,155 (65 per cent.) from Great Britain. Exports, £932,773, of which £370,356 (40 per cent.) to Great Britain.

Sierra Leone buys from Britain more than twice the amount she sells.

Tariff preference to Great Britain is given over a range of imported goods. In some cases British goods are admitted duty free, while foreign goods are charged a 10 per cent. duty. In other cases British goods pay a fifth or a quarter less than the general tariff rate.

British Somaliland

A protectorate on the East Coast of Africa, on the south shore of the Gulf of Aden. Declared a British protectorate in 1884.

Area, 68,000 square miles. Population, 344,700. Chief town, Berbera.

The chief products are cattle, sheep, goats, hides, and skins.

Trade in 1932: Imports, £306,634, of which £15,600 (5 per cent.) from Great Britain. Exports, £160,254, of which £44,000 (28 per cent.) to Great Britain.

The protectorate gives preferences to a limited range of British goods. Where the general tariff rate is 25 per cent., the preferential tariff is 15 per cent.

The Sudan

An Anglo-Egyptian condominium since the Anglo-Egyptian conquest of 1896–8. Extending from the southern boundary of Egypt to the northern boundary of Uganda and watered by the Nile.

Area, 1,008,000 square miles. Population, 5,600,000, including 3,000 Europeans. Adminis-

tered by a Governor-General, aided by a nominated
Council. Capital, Khartoum.

The principal grain crop is millet, which is the
staple food of the people. Egyptian cotton has
been introduced, and production of this is capable
of great extension. The Gezira irrigation scheme
enables an area of 681,000 acres to be cultivated.
Railways, 1,989 miles.

Trade in 1932: Imports, £E3,054,644, of which
£E692,623 (22 per cent.) from Great Britain.
Exports, £E3,797,528, of which £E2,667,099 (70
per cent.) to Great Britain. Cotton accounts for
37 per cent. of the total export.

The Egyptian pound (£E) is approximately
equal in value to the pound sterling.

The Sudan sells to Britain almost four times
the amount she buys from Britain.

No duties may be levied on imports from Egypt,
and duties on imports entering the Red Sea ports
may not exceed those levied in Egypt. This means
that the Sudan tariff is regulated by the commercial treaties of Egypt with other countries.

Swaziland

A native protectorate in South Africa, lying
between the Transvaal and Portuguese East
Africa. Administered by a High Commissioner,
who is the Governor-General of South Africa.

Area, 6,705 square miles. Population, 112,981,
of whom 2,205 are whites. Headquarters of
Administration, Mbabane.

The whole territory provides excellent grazing
for cattle, of which there are 346,772 head.
Maize, tobacco, and millet are grown. Cotton
growing is becoming important. The mineral
wealth (tin, gold, coal, and copper) is considerable.
Omnibus services cover 222 miles.

In 1931, Swaziland imported £3,933 of goods
from the United Kingdom and exported £600 to it.

Swaziland is dealt with as part of the Union of South Africa for Customs purposes.

Tanganyika

A mandated territory of East Africa, bounded on the north by Kenya and on the south by Northern Rhodesia, Nyasaland, and Portuguese East Africa. Has a coastline 500 miles long on the Indian Ocean.

Area, 373,500 square miles. Population, 4,933,000 natives and 8,150 whites. A former German colony now administered under a League of Nations mandate. Capital, Dar-es-Salaam.

There are 4,000 square miles of forest, 5,336,000 cattle, 2,281,000 sheep, and 3,374,000 goats.

The European-owned plantations produce sisal fibre and coffee, with smaller areas under tea and tobacco. Minerals found include gold, salt, mica, and tin. Railways, 2,265 miles.

Trade in 1932: Imports, £1,871,992, of which £421,322 (22 per cent.) from Great Britain. Exports, £2,199,216, of which £652,322 (30 per cent.) to Great Britain.

Tanganyika sells to Britain 50 per cent. more than she buys.

Under the terms of the mandate, Tanganyika cannot give tariff preference to British imports.

Uganda

A protectorate in East Africa, acquired by cession in 1894. The native kings are encouraged to conduct the government of their own subjects, but the British Governor, with the aid of Executive and Legislative Councils, makes ordinances for the administration of justice.

Area, 94,204 square miles, of which 13,616 are water. Population, 3,553,534, of whom 2,000 are Europeans. Capital, Entebbe.

The production for exports consists chiefly of cotton, coffee, oil-seeds, rubber, ivory, and tin ore.

Trade in 1931: Imports, £1,308,726. Exports, £1,978,262.

Uganda, by the Congo Basin Treaty, cannot give tariff preference to British imports.

Zanzibar

A protectorate off the East Coast of Africa, consisting of the islands of Zanzibar and Pemba, of smaller islands, and of a coastal strip, which, however, is under the administration of the British Government.

The British protectorate dates from 1890.

Area, 1,020 square miles. Population, 235,428. Capital, Zanzibar, the largest city in Eastern Africa.

Zanzibar possesses practically a monopoly in cloves, and also produces copra. It serves as an important distributing centre for the East African coast.

Trade in 1932: Imports, £944,814, of which £133,293 (14 per cent.) from Great Britain. Exports: £910,267, of which £63,343 (7 per cent.) to Great Britain.

Zanzibar buys twice as much from Britain as she sells.

Zanzibar is one of the territories which, under the Congo Basin Treaty (see p. 84) are precluded from giving tariff preferences to British imports.

V

CROWN COLONIES IN WEST ATLANTIC

The Bahamas

An archipelago of the British West Indies extending from the Coast of Florida to Haiti. Settled in 1629. Government vested in a Governor, with an Executive Council and a nominated Legislative Council. There are 20 inhabited islands and a large number of islets and rocks.

Area, 4,404 square miles. Population, 61,812, mostly the descendants of freed negro slaves. Capital, Nassau.

The chief crops are corn, sisal hemp, and tomatoes. The last is the most important industry, the export in 1932 being worth £78,000.

Trade in 1932: Imports, £940,354, of which £228,336 (24 per cent.) from the United Kingdom. Exports, £263,886, of which £23,370 (9 per cent.) to the United Kingdom. In 1929 50 per cent. of the exports went to the United States and 14 per cent. to Canada.

The Bahamas buy from Britain ten times the amount they sell.

They give a preference to British imports, amounting to one-quarter of the duty.

Barbados

The most easterly of the West Indian islands. Settled 1625. Governed by a Governor and nominated Legislative Council.

Area, 106,000 acres. Population, 176,874. Capital, Bridgetown.

A quarter of the island is under sugar-cane, and

three-quarters of the export trade consists of sugar.

Trade in 1932: Imports, £1,656,876, of which £763,581 (46 per cent.) from United Kingdom. Exports, £1,379,006, of which £324,807 (25 per cent.) to the United Kingdom.

The Barbados buy from Britain more than twice the amount they sell to Britain.

In 1929, 80 per cent. of the exports went to Canada.

The preferential tariff on British goods is 50 per cent. of that levied on foreign imports.

Bermuda

A group of 100 small islands (only 15 inhabited) in the Atlantic Ocean, 580 miles from the North Carolina Coast. Colonized in 1609. Government is in the hands of a Governor and Legislative Council, appointed by the Crown.

Area, 20 square miles. Population, 27,789, of whom 11,353 are white. Capital, Hamilton.

The colony specializes in producing vegetables for the United States market, the whole export trade consisting of vegetables, flowers, and bulbs.

Trade in 1932: Imports, £1,891,526, of which £717,213 (38 per cent.) from the United Kingdom. Exports, £145,950, of which £6,263 to the United Kingdom.

Bermuda buys from Britain over a hundred times the amount she sells.

In 1930, 26 per cent. of the imports came from the United Kingdom, 27 per cent. from Canada, and 45 per cent. from the United States. Of the exports, 15 per cent. went to United Kingdom, 14 per cent. to Canada, and 51 per cent. to the United States.

In the Bermuda tariff, a preference is given to British imports by means of a surtax amounting to one-quarter of the duty on all dutiable articles from foreign countries.

Falkland Islands

A group of islands in the South Atlantic, 300 miles east of the Strait of Magellan. Acquired, 1833. Dependencies: South Georgia (area, 1,094 square miles), with a population engaged in whaling; South Shetlands, and South Orkneys.

Area of the Falkland Islands, 4,618 square miles. Population, 2,428. Capital, Port Stanley.

The islands are suitable for sheep-rearing. Sheep, 615,767. Chief exports are wool and sheep-skins. The whaling industry in the dependencies is greater than that of the rest of the world combined.

Trade in 1932: Imports, £186,802, of which £95,443 from Great Britain. Exports, £481,364, of which £238,750 to Great Britain.

Duties on Empire imports are charged at nine-tenths of the general rate.

British Guiana

A Crown colony on the north-east coast of South America. Acquired by conquest and cession between 1803 and 1814. There is a Legislative Council, with 10 official and 19 unofficial members.

Area, 89,480 square miles. Population, 317,813, of whom 134,059 are East Indian immigrants. Capital, Georgetown.

The principal crop of the colony is sugar-cane, which accounts for a quarter of the total area under British cultivation. Rice is next in importance.

About 90 per cent. of the whole area of the colony is covered by forests of both hardwood and softwood, but 80 per cent. are at present inaccessible. The chief exports are sugar, diamonds, rice, and the aluminium clay, bauxite. Railways, 95 miles.

Trade in 1932: Imports, £1,690,891, of which

£1,078,278 (60 per cent.) from the United Kingdom. Exports, £2,208,901, of which £1,007,649 (45 per cent.) to the United Kingdom.

In 1930, 57 per cent. of the total imports came from the United Kingdom, 16 per cent. from Canada, and 11 per cent. from the United States. Exports, 30 per cent. to the United Kingdom, 39 per cent. to Canada.

The tariff rebate on Empire goods is generally half of the general rate of duty.

British Honduras

A Crown colony on the mainland of Central America. Conquered 1798.

Area, 8,598 square miles. Population, 51,347. Capital, Belize.

The country consists chiefly of primeval forests, and its staple products are mahogany, cedar, and logwood. Chicle, a resinous substance used in the manufacture of chewing-gum, is also obtained from the forests.

The chief agricultural products are coco-nuts, bananas, sugar, and citrus fruits.

In September 1931 a disastrous hurricane devastated the capital of the colony, with a loss of nearly 1,000 lives.

Trade in 1932: Imports, £460,300, of which £85,000 (18 per cent.) from Great Britain. Exports, £289,000, of which £12,600 (4 per cent.) to Great Britain. (These values are converted to British currency at par.)

In 1930, 14 per cent. of the imports came from Britain and 35 per cent. from the United States. Exports: 8 per cent. to Britain, 28 per cent. to British West Indies, and 60 per cent. to the United States.

British Honduras buys from Britain substantially more than she sells to Britain.

The tariff preference on Empire imports usually amounts to one-half of the general duty.

Jamaica

A Crown colony in the West Indies, conquered from the Spaniards in 1655.

Area, 4,450 square miles. Population, 858,118, of which 14,476 are whites. The Captain-General is assisted by a Privy Council and a Legislative Council with an official majority. Capital, Kingston.

The principal crop is bananas, which is also the chief export. The acreage under coco-nuts is as large as that under sugar, each being half the acreage under bananas. Coffee growing has declined. Railways, 210 miles.

The Cayman Islands (population, 6,182) and Turk and Caicos Islands (population, 5,612), both dependencies of Jamaica, produce turtle shell and sponges.

Trade of Jamaica in 1932: Imports, £4,754,152, of which £1,890,526 (40 per cent.) from the United Kingdom. Exports, £3,271,357, of which £1,570,528 (50 per cent.) to the United Kingdom.

Jamaica buys more from Britain than she sells to Britain.

In 1930, 28 per cent. of the Jamaican imports came from the United Kingdom, 16 per cent. from Canada, and 32 per cent. from the United States.

The Jamaican preferential duty on British imports is 75 per cent. of the general tariff rate.

Jamaica, with the Gold Coast and Nigeria, provides the best opportunity for the expansion of British trade in the Crown colonies.

The Leeward Islands

A Federal Crown colony of the West Indies, consisting of:

1. Antigua and Barbuda (population, 32,144).
2. St. Kitts and Nevis (population, 36,730).
3. Dominica (population, 44,103).

4. Montserrat (population, 12,880).

5. The Virgin Islands (population, 5,082).

Total area, 718 square miles. Total population, 131,000.

The most important crop is sugar-cane, but vegetables, limes, cotton, and coco-nuts are also grown.

Trade in 1931: Total imports, £619,000, of which £210,000 from the United Kingdom and £139,000 from Canada. Exports, £285,242, of which £81,990 to the United Kingdom and £128,560 to Canada.

The Leeward Islands buy twice as much from Britain as they sell to Britain.

The preferential duty on British imports is generally two-thirds of the general duty.

Trinidad and Tobago

Trinidad, the most southerly of the West Indies, is 7 miles from the coast of Venezuela. Captured from the Spaniards, 1797. There is a Legislative Council with a nominated majority.

Area, 1,862 square miles (Tobago, 114 square miles). Population, including Tobago, 419,559. Capital, Port of Spain.

The chief crop is cocoa (210,000 acres). Cultivation of sugar-cane comes next. Forests, 700,000 acres. Most of the timber cut is used in the colony. Trinidad is the most important mineral-oil producer in the Empire (40 per cent. of the whole). There is an asphalt lake 110 acres in extent.

Trade in 1932: Imports, £3,695,137, of which £1,583,000 (42 per cent.) from Great Britain. Exports, £4,156,211, of which £1,155,000 (28 per cent.) to Great Britain. In 1930, 25 per cent. of the imports of Trinidad came from the United States and 15 per cent. from Canada.

The British preferential tariff is generally half the general rate.

The Windward Islands

The three West Indian colonies of Grenada, St. Vincent, and St. Lucia are united under one Governor, but each retains its own institutions.

Area, 508 square miles. Population, 162,254.

The soil of Grenada is fertile; principal crop, cocoa. St. Vincent is the world's largest supplier of arrowroot. Cocoa is the chief crop of St. Lucia.

Trade in 1932: Total imports of the Windward Islands, £574,301, of which £271,047 (47 per cent.) from the United Kingdom. Exports, £403,725, of which £159,736 (39 per cent.) to the United Kingdom.

The preferential duty on British goods is generally a third less than the general rate.

VI

CROWN COLONIES IN ASIA

Borneo

The State of North Borneo occupies the northern part of this large island of the Eastern Archipelago. It is a British protectorate (ceded 1877), administered by the British North Borneo Company.

Area, 31,000 square miles. Population, 270,223. Capital, Sandakan.

The chief products are timber, tobacco, rubber, and copra. Timber accounts for two-fifths of the exports; tobacco and rubber for about a tenth each.

Trade in 1932: Imports, £390,000. Exports, £677,000.

Brunei is a native State in Borneo under British protection since 1888.

Area, 2,500 square miles. Population, 30,135. Capital, Brunei.

Trade in 1932: Imports, £283,529. Exports, £175,669. The chief exports are rubber and sago.

In North Borneo, a 25 per cent. rebate of duty is given to British goods on eleven items of trade. In Brunei a few preferences are given.

Ceylon

An island to the south-east of India. Taken from the Dutch, 1796.

Area, 25,332 square miles. Population, 5,312,548. Capital, Colombo.

The government is administered by the Governor, aided by a State Council, in which there is an elected majority of 50 members, with 8 nominated members and 3 officers of State.

About a fifth of the island is cultivated: tea, 457,000 acres; rubber, 534,000 acres. The chief exports are tea, rubber, coco-nut, palm products, and plumbago. Ceylon sells a considerable amount of tea to Australia and New Zealand. Railways, 951 miles.

Trade in 1932: Imports, £15,100,000, of which £2,874,000 (19 per cent.) from Great Britain. Exports, £13,100,000, of which £6,457,000 (49 per cent.) to Great Britain.

Ceylon sells to Britain more than twice the amount she buys from Britain.

A preferential rebate of two-fifths or one-half is given on a variety of Empire goods entering the colony.

The Ceylon State Council has so far declined to ratify the Ottawa Agreement imposing preferential duties on cotton piece-goods.

Hong Kong

A Crown colony off the coast of China, at the mouth of the Canton River. Ceded, 1842.

Area, 391 square miles. Population, 900,796. Capital, Victoria.

Hong Kong is the centre of a vast shipping trade. Tonnage entering in 1932, 22 millions.

Trade in 1932: Imports from United Kingdom, £5,046,915. Exports to United Kingdom, £227,210.

Malaya

British Malaya consists of the Straits Settlements, the four Federated Malay States, which federated under British protection in 1895, and the five Unfederated Malay States, the last of which came under British protection in 1909.

The total area of Malaya is 51,000 square miles.

Population, 4,206,980, including 16,688 Europeans.

(1) *The Straits Settlements* include the great island seaport of Singapore, founded 1819 by Sir Stamford Raffles (tonnage entering Singapore, 1932, 28 millions); Penang, another important emporium; Malacca, which became a British possession in 1824; Labuan, and some small islands. There is a Legislative Council, with a nominated majority.

(2) *The Federated Malay States* of Perak, Selangor, Negri Sembilan, and Pahang on the Malay Peninsula are administered under the advice of the British chief secretary, subject to the instructions of the High Commissioner, who is also the Governor of the Straits Settlements.

(3) *The Unfederated Malay States.*—In Johore, the Sultan has, since 1888, accepted the advice of a British official called the General Adviser. Kedah, Perlis, Kelantan, and Trengganu are also British protectorates, the reigning Raja or Sultan of which takes British advice.

Malaya is the largest producer of rubber and tin in the world. There are 3 million acres under rubber. Rice, coco-nuts, and pineapples are also important. There is as much land devoted to pine-apple growing as in Hawaii, the other great centre of the industry. Tin ore production equals 37 per cent. of the world's output.

Railways, 1,187 miles.

Trade in 1932: Imports, £43,957,457, of which £6,425,762 (14 per cent.) from Great Britain and £7,829,373 from other British countries. Exports, £37,730,367, of which £4,204,844 (11 per cent.) to Great Britain and £6,998,313 to other British countries.

Malaya buys more from Britain than she sells to Britain.

In 1930, rubber accounted for 36 per cent. and tin for 18 per cent. of the total exports of Malaya. Sixty per cent. of the rubber and 59 per cent. of the tin went to the United States, whose share of the total export trade of Malaya was 34 per cent.

There is a preferential tariff in the Federated Malay States, giving an advantage to Empire goods of from one-tenth to one-half of the duty on a number of articles.

Sarawak

A State on the north-west coast of Borneo.

Area, 50,000 square miles. Population, 475,000. Capital, Kuching.

The government was taken over in 1843 from the Sultan of Brunei by Sir James Brooke, who became Raja of Sarawak. In 1888 the State was placed under British protection. Government is in the hands of the Raja and a Supreme Council of 4 Europeans and 5 Malay magistrates.

The country produces oil, sago, rubber, and pepper.

Trade in 1932: Imports, £1,141,000, of which £40,000 from Great Britain. Exports, £1,600,000, of which £220,000 to Great Britain (13 per cent.).

Sarawak sells to Britain five times as much as she buys from Britain.

Tariff preferences are given to British goods on a few classes of manufactured articles.

VII

OTHER COLONIES

Channel Islands

Situated off the north-west coast of France. The only portions of the Dukedom of Normandy now belonging to Britain. They consist of Jersey, Guernsey, Alderney, Sark, and smaller islands.

Area, 75 square miles. Population, 93,197. Chief town: of Jersey, St. Helier; of Guernsey, St. Peter Port.

The principal officer in each island is the Lieut.-Governor, who represents the King as Duke of Normandy. French, the language of the people, is also the official language of the local legislatures, called States.

There is a considerable production of potatoes, tomatoes, and flowers. Most of the trade is with Great Britain.

The trade with Britain in 1933 was: Imports, £4,345,000. Exports, £4,433,000.

The Channel Islands have adopted the same customs tariff as the United Kingdom.

Cyprus

An island colony in the Eastern Mediterranean, 60 miles from the Syrian coast. Formally annexed to the Empire in 1914. Power to legislate is vested in the Governor.

Area, 3,584 square miles. Population, 347,959, 18 per cent. Moslems, the rest mainly members of the Greek Orthodox Church. Capital, Nicosia.

The main products are grain, sesame, linseed, flax, wine, silk, and olives.

Trade in 1932: Imports, £1,347,288, of which
£386,675 (29 per cent.) from Great Britain.
Exports, £922,426, of which £276,959 (30 per cent.)
to Britain.

Tariff preference is given on British imports.
It varies between one-sixth and two-thirds of the
duty on foreign imports.

Fiji

A group of 200 islands in the South Pacific.
Ceded, 1874.

Area, 7,083 square miles. Population, 189,398,
of whom 4,863 are Europeans. Capital, Suva.

There is a considerable cultivation of bananas,
sugar, fruit, and vegetables.

Trade in 1932: Imports, £857,346, of which
£250,748 (29 per cent.) from Great Britain. Exports, £1,698,964, of which £847,053 (50 per cent.)
to Great Britain.

Fiji sells substantially more to Britain than she
buys from Britain.

Fiji gives preferences to British imports over
a wide range of articles. Generally, the preferential tariff is about half the general rate.

Gibraltar

A rocky promontory near the southern extremity
of Spain. Captured from the Spaniards, 1704.
Civilian population, 16,009. The Governor is in
command of the garrison.

Gibraltar is a free port. In 1932, $8\frac{1}{2}$ million
tons of shipping entered.

Empire preferences are given on a few articles.

Malta

An island colony in the Mediterranean, 58 miles
from Sicily. Captured from the French, 1800.

Area, 91½ square miles. Civil population, 241,621. Capital, Valetta.

The legislature is composed of a Senate (17 members) and a Legislative Assembly (32 members returned by 8 electoral districts). In November 1933, the Governor dismissed the Ministry and assumed the emergency powers vested in them by the Constitution.

The island is closely cultivated, vegetables and fruits of many kinds being grown.

The principal harbour of Valetta is one of the finest in the world. There is an arsenal and dockyard, Malta being the headquarters of the Mediterranean Fleet.

Trade in 1931: Imports, £3,712,530, of which £1,131,000 (30 per cent.) from Great Britain. Exports, £499,055, of which £38,000 (8 per cent.) to Great Britain.

No tariff preference is given to British imports.

Mauritius

An island in the Indian Ocean, 550 miles east of Madagascar.

Area, 720 square miles. Population (Indians, Europeans, mainly French, and natives), 393,418. Capital, Port Louis, population, 54,000.

Captured from the French, 1810. French language and law used. One hundred and forty-four miles of railway. Total cultivated area, 170,000 acres, of which 135,000 are under sugar.

Trade in 1931: Imports, £2,454,500, of which £562,800 (23 per cent.) from United Kingdom, £1,175,000 from Empire, and £710,700 from foreign countries. Exports, £1,720,800, of which £1,496,800 (87 per cent.) to United Kingdom, £210,000 to Empire, and £13,759 to foreign countries.

Mauritius imports more from foreign countries

than from the United Kingdom. Her chief foreign sources of imports are France, Japan, and the United States. Her exports are almost exclusively to the United Kingdom, and, except for a small amount of fibres, consist only of raw sugar (3,500 cwts., value £1,669,000, in 1931).

Mauritius is a Crown colony, with a Governor, who is aided by an Executive Council of 4 official and other nominated members, and a Legislative Council of 27 (8 official, 9 nominated, 10 elected).

The tariff of Mauritius is authorized by Ordinance No. 28 of 1932. The existing tariff gives preferences to the *United Kingdom and Canada*, and the Governor may, by proclamation, extend them to other British territories granting reciprocity. Under this power the preferences on hams, bacon, and cheese were extended to Australia in 1933. Note that Mauritius sells all her exports to the United Kingdom, but buys only one-fifth of her imports from the United Kingdom.

Pacific Islands

These island groups in the Pacific Ocean are:

(1) *The Solomon Islands*, a protectorate since 1893. Area, 11,000 square miles. Population, 94,000.

(2) *The Gilbert and Ellice Islands*, annexed to the Empire, 1915. Area, 180 square miles. Population, 34,000.

(3) *The Tonga* or *Friendly Islands.*—A protectorate since 1900. Area, 358 square miles. Population, 29,454.

(4) *The New Hebrides*, administered by a Franco-British Condominium Government. Area, 5,700 square miles. Population, 43,000.

There are also the Phœnix Islands, Pitcairn Island, and smaller groups.

Trade in 1932: Imports, £1,403,809, of which £295,064 (21 per cent.) from the United Kingdom. Exports, £2,786,269, of which £847,053 (30 per cent.) to the United Kingdom.

The purchases of these islands from Britain are thus considerably smaller than their sales to Britain.

Palestine

A mandated territory since 1923.

Area, 10,000 square miles. Population, 1,031,821, of whom 759,712 are Moslems, 174,610 Jews, and 91,398 Christians. Capital, Jerusalem.

Since 1920, about 118,000 immigrants, mostly Jews, have entered the country.

The colonization of Palestine by the Jews, in accordance with the policy of making the country a " National Home " for the Hebrew people, has led to frequent, sometimes dangerous, disturbances. The mandate has imposed upon Britain grave and expensive responsibilities, which seem likely to grow as the Jewish population increases, and with it, the feeling of resentment among dispossessed Arabs.

According to figures given by Mr. Ramsay MacDonald, the British Treasury had paid £14,429,000 to Palestine up to 1924. Since then, grants-in-aid amounting to £869,074 have been given, and an advance from the Colonial Development Fund of £27,754.

The British Government backed the Palestine Loan, 1927, for £4,475,000, and another loan in 1934 of £2 millions.

The industrial and agricultural development of the country has gone ahead with great speed in recent years. The cultivation of oranges and other fruits has been exploited with particular energy. Railways, 670 miles.

Trade in 1932: Imports, £8,120,797, of which £1,342,031 (16 per cent.) from Great Britain. Exports, £4,327,426, of which £1,522,073 (35 per cent.) to Great Britain.

Under the terms of the Mandate, Palestine does not give preferences to British imports.

St. Helena

A solitary island colony in the South Atlantic, 1,140 miles from the nearest point of the African Continent. Seized by the East India Company in 1673.

Area, 47 square miles. Population, 3,995. Capital, Jamestown.

Trade in 1932: Imports, £36,229, of which £28,732 from Great Britain. Exports, £6,880, of which £5,774 to Great Britain.

Seychelles

The Seychelles Islands, in the Indian Ocean, were captured by the British in 1794, and erected into a separate colony 1903. There are five principal islands—Mahe, Praslin, Silhouette, Curieuse, and La Digue.

Area, 156 square miles. Population, 28,235. Capital, Victoria.

The chief exports are copra, vanilla, coco-nuts, and tortoise-shells.

Trade in 1932: Imports, £80,000, of which £21,000 (25 per cent.) came from the United Kingdom. Exports, £104,000 of which £27,000 (26 per cent.) to the United Kingdom.

The preferential rate on British imports into the Seychelles is generally three-fifths of the general rate of duty.

Tristan da Cunha

A tiny isolated colony in the South Atlantic, 2,000 miles west of the Cape of Good Hope.

Annexed in 1816. Population, 163.

The main settlement, Edinburgh, is in a fertile tract in the north-west of the island.

Until 1933 the oldest inhabitant acted as governor, then a council of four was set up.

VIII

HISTORY OF THE EMPIRE FREE TRADE MOVEMENT

The Empire policy was first launched as a definite political campaign in Britain by Joseph Chamberlain in 1903.

It was renewed, renamed, and reshaped to suit the changed conditions of the times in 1929. I called the policy "Empire Free Trade," a name now in general use.

The policy is built upon the structure which Joseph Chamberlain erected in 1903. But there is one important respect in which Empire Free Trade, as I submitted it to the people, goes beyond the Chamberlain policy of "Imperial Preferences."

Empire Free Trade is not content to envisage a system of preferential tariffs within the Empire. Its ideal is that of a progressive advance towards complete freedom of trade, unimpeded by duty or customs barrier of any description, between Britain, the Dominions, and the Crown colonies.

I was joined by Sir Hugo Cunliffe-Owen and Mr. C. A. McCurdy. They raised money for me, and enabled me to launch what soon became famous as the Empire Crusade.

Lord Rothermere brought to the cause the unparalleled support of his great personal prestige in our public life and the vast influence of his newspapers.

From another source strong assistance came. The "Norfolk Movement," organized among farmers in Norfolk by Mr. J. F. Wright, soon became the spearhead of the movement in agricultural Britain for the imposition of duties on imported foreign foodstuffs.

There was a unity of purpose between the
Empire Crusade and the farmers' movement,
which came to have a position of acknowledged
leadership in the farming community. Both
wanted to exclude foreign foodstuffs by tariff from
the British market. The alliance between them
brought strength to both.

After a series of crucial by-elections, in which
with one exception the Empire Free Trade candidate outstripped the candidate put forward by
Conservative Headquarters, there came acceptance
of the Empire policy on the part of the Conservative Party. This took place in March 1931.

After the General Election of 1931, when a
National Coalition Government, of a predominantly
Conservative character, came into power, the supporters of the Empire policy had the right to
presume that their principles would be carried
into effect. They were subjected to a bitter dis-
appointment. The policy was not put into
practice.

The Ottawa agreements with the Dominions were
only an insignificant advance in the direction of
the Empire Free Trade goal. The refusal of the
Government to impose taxes on foreign meat in-
terposed an insuperable barrier to the accomplish-
ment of the policy.

The Empire Crusade is faced by two chief
obstacles:

(1) The existence of treaties with foreigners
which prevent the establishment of Empire Free
Trade over great areas of the African colonies.

(2) The propaganda skilfully disseminated in
rural districts by Ministerial supporters, in order
to create the impression that the Dominions are
interfering with the protection of British agriculture. This propaganda has been momentarily and
partially successful. But it can be countered. It
is based on a misapprehension.

It springs from the failure—or the refusal—to understand that there is ample room in the British market for the home producer and the Dominion producer, provided the foreigner is excluded.

This failure of understanding is due to the Government's determination to ride two horses, the Empire horse and the foreign horse. Important circles in Britain are interested, for natural and honourable but quite selfish motives, in trade with foreign countries.

But the Government must declare to win with one horse. It should be the Empire horse, carrying the owner's colours!

The supporters of our policy were heartened by an impressive rally of public indignation following on the Government's attitude to a question which was regarded by us as tantamount to an offer of Empire Free Trade from New Zealand. As the weeks and the months go by, new opportunities for advancing the Empire cause will appear.

The Crusade goes on, and will go on, until the goal is reached!

IX

THE EFFECT OF THE OTTAWA AGREEMENTS

At the Imperial Economic Conference, held in Ottawa in the summer of 1932, a series of agreements was concluded between Britain and the various dominions.

These agreements conferred on Britain some limited but useful tariff preferences in the dominions in exchange for freedom from any quantitative restrictions imposed by Britain on agricultural imports and a few small additions to the British tariffs.

The way to a fuller realization of the Empire Free Trade policy was barred by the refusal of the British Government to entertain proposals for the taxation of foreign meat imports into Great Britain.

But the Ottawa agreements were a small advance along the road of Imperial Preferences towards Empire Free Trade. Let us see what effect, if any, they have had on Britain's import and export trade.

If the year 1931 be compared with 1933, the first full year of trading under the Ottawa agreements, it is found that Britain's exports to the dominions increased by nearly £14 millions, while our imports from them increased by £16½ millions.

The proportion of our exports to the dominions rose from 18 per cent. of the total export trade to 22 per cent., while our imports from the dominions rose from 15 per cent. in 1931 to 22 per cent. in 1933.

In these figures the trade with the Irish Free

State is ignored, as no agreement was concluded with the Irish Free State at Ottawa.

Ottawa made no difference to our fiscal relations with the Crown colonies, but as these get free entry for their goods into the British market while a large number of competing foreign commodities are subject to duties, a survey of the British trade figures for 1931 and 1933 may be expected to reflect this fact.

The export to the Crown colonies remained stationary, but as the total export trade had fallen by £23 millions, there was a trifling rise, from $9\frac{1}{2}$ to 10 per cent., in the proportion of the total British exports which went to the colonies.

Imports from the Crown colonies were also stationary, but the percentage of the total trade rose from 5 to $6\frac{1}{2}$.

X

NEW ZEALAND'S ENQUIRY

On October 25th, 1933, Mr. Forbes, Prime Minister of New Zealand, sent the following message to the British Government:

" There is a widespread belief, on the part of producers in New Zealand, that if we undertook a drastic reduction or removal of New Zealand's protective tariff on United Kingdom goods, His Majesty's Government in the United Kingdom would guarantee continuance of unrestricted entry of New Zealand primary products. His Majesty's Government in New Zealand would be grateful if His Majesty's Government in the United Kingdom would indicate their attitude towards this suggestion."

Two months after receiving the message, Mr. J. H. Thomas, Secretary for Dominion Affairs, replied on behalf of the British Government:

" The suggestion in your telegram would involve modification of United Kingdom policy (i.e. of Quotas), and could hardly be considered with reference to New Zealand alone. Nor we think could an examination of such a question take place on the basis of a suggestion put forward by particular trade interests."

When these communications were published in April 1934, it was realized that an important new chapter in Empire history had been dramatically opened.

It was maintained by those who favoured the Empire Free Trade cause, and by Liberals who opposed the Government, that New Zealand had made an offer of Empire Free Trade to Britain, and had been flouted by the British Government.

The British Ministers and their supporters, however, held that the New Zealand Prime Minister had made no offer at all, that he had merely put out an enquiry owing to pressure from his dairy producers, and that New Zealand, in any case, could not afford to deprive herself of the revenue from her customs duties on British imports.

To these arguments the Empire Free Traders replied by saying that if Mr. Forbes was not sincere in putting forward his offer, Mr. Thomas should have called his bluff. If Mr. Forbes had been compelled to make the offer by the pressure of public opinion in New Zealand, that was all the more reason for Mr. Thomas to take it seriously.

Considerable public feeling was roused by the publication of the documents, and the Empire Free Trade movement received a powerful stimulus.

It was revealed in the *Daily Express* that in the six months ending February 1934, the import of butter from foreign countries increased by 169,000 cwts., while imports from British countries increased by only 69,000 cwts. This weakened the pretensions of the Anti-Empire element that the British farmer needed protection against the dominions.

Mr. Fulton, of the New Zealand Dairy Board, who was in Britain at the time, revealed that the foreign butter against which New Zealand was competing was subsidized.

Dutch butter was selling in Holland at 150*s.* a cwt., while the export price was 50*s.* Danish butter cost £10 per 100 kilos in Denmark and £6 for export.

AUSTRALIA AND EMPIRE FREE TRADE

In April 1934, Mr. Bruce, Australian High Commissioner in London, on a visit to Australia, said that Australia should limit her exports of meat to the British market. If Australia and New Zealand indiscriminately exported mutton and lamb, Great Britain would inevitably impose restrictions to protect her own farmers.

In relation to butter, he said that Australia should not wait for the Ottawa agreements to expire, but should make a new agreement stabilizing her export to Britain.

The Bruce policy of voluntary restrictions of exports undertaken to anticipate the imposition of quotas by Britain, met with strong opposition in Australia. The Australian Country Party, who carry the Empire banner in the Commonwealth, said: " Mr. Bruce's policy of a restriction of trade with Britain is suicidal to both ends of the Empire. Australia should give increased preferences to Britain. But Britain, in return, should permit Australian products to enter freely."

Mr. Bruce said that, even if Australian tariff barriers against Britain were removed, the Australians could not gain unrestricted entry for their products into Britain.

He added that New Zealand's unfortunate position has proved that a reduction of the Australian tariff would not induce Britain to alter her policy.

Mr. Lyons, the Prime Minister of Australia, then announced that Australia would not regulate her beef and butter exports unless it were absolutely necessary.

XII

RHODESIA'S "LAST OFFER"

The British Government's policy of imposing quotas on imports of primary products from the dominions embroiled New Zealand and Australia with the mother country.

Then came a startling speech by Mr. G. M. Huggins, Prime Minister of Southern Rhodesia, in April 1934. He said that if Britain refused a reasonable place in her market to the colonies, they would have nothing but a sentimental attachment towards Britain. They would be compelled to make agreements with other countries.

"Now is the time for Britain to decide," he declared. "Rhodesia could take hundreds of thousands of settlers if the Home Government guaranteed a place in her markets. Britain now has another chance, but it is the very last."

The publication of this speech in the *Daily Express* and other British newspapers aroused the nation to a fresh sense of the dangers involved in the policy the Government had adopted towards the dominions.

The British Government, it was evident, was endeavouring to pursue two contradictory policies at the same time. It was trying to expand foreign trade by means of its trade agreements with foreign countries. It was also trying to develop Empire trade. The two policies could not be reconciled. The Government must plainly choose between them.

AN OFFER BY JAMAICA REJECTED

In the summer of 1933, the Jamaican Legislature, alarmed by the dumping of Japanese cotton goods into the island, cabled a Resolution to the Secretary for the Colonies.

The vital passage of the Resolution read as follows:

> " This Council therefore desires to state that Jamaica would be willing to co-operate with Britain and other parts of the Empire for an expansion of wider reciprocal trade."

In his reply, the Secretary for the Colonies said that the Board of Trade urged that no legislation in Jamaica should take place until the outcome of negotiations with the Japanese. His reply went on:

> " It has been decided for the present to confine termination of application of Anglo-Japanese Commercial Treaty to West African Dependencies, where special complications of Anglo-French Convention exist."

Jamaican opinion was annoyed by the rebuff. The *Daily Gleaner*, published in Kingston, Jamaica, printed the news with the heading:

> " Secretary of State orders hands-off policy in respect of goods from land of Nippon."

Members of the Jamaican Legislature repeatedly urged through the autumn of 1933 that action be taken against the Japanese dumpers.

But when Britain finally sought the co-operation
of Jamaica and other Crown colonies in May 1934,
the method imposed on the colonies was quotas,
which made it impossible for the colonies to collect
revenue by means of increased duties on Japanese
imports.

XIV

JAPANESE COTTON IMPORTS INTO BRITISH CROWN COLONIES

The serious growth in Japanese imports of cotton piece-goods and artificial silk into the Crown colonies compelled the British Government in May 1934 to impose a quota system for these goods in part of the Colonial Empire.

The quota is to be fixed on the average Japanese imports over the years 1927–31.

In these years the average Japanese imports were 87·7 million square yards. By 1932 this had increased to 205 million square yards, and by 1933 to 222 million square yards—a growth of 150 per cent.

Lancashire's export trade to the Crown colonies, owing to the Japanese competition, declined from 307 million square yards in 1932 to 191·5 million square yards in 1933—a fall of 38 per cent.

The position in some of the larger colonies is:

Cotton Piece-Goods

In million sq. yards.

	Average over the basic years for quota 1927–31.	1933.
Imports of Ceylon:		
From Great Britain	24.2	9.6
From Japan	11.7	41.4
Imports of British Malaya:		
From Great Britain	57.3	25.8
From Japan	39.9	99.6
Imports of British East Africa:		
From Great Britain	14.6	8.5
From Japan	28.6	65.2

In contrast with these figures should be set the facts relating to Japanese trade in cotton piece-goods with the possessions of foreign Powers where conditions approximating to Empire Free Trade exist.

The Japanese imports of cotton piece-goods into the *Philippine Islands,* an American possession, fell from 31 per cent. of the total import in 1931 to 18 per cent. in 1932. In the same years, the import from the United States rose from 49 per cent. to 63 per cent.

In *Porto Rico,* also an American colony, there is practically no foreign import of cotton piece-goods. In the year ending July 1932, the foreign imports were worth only $36,000, while the Americans had an import of $8 millions.

In *Hawaii* there was a fall of 40 per cent. in piece-goods imports from Japan between 1931 and 1932.

In *French Indo-China* the import of cotton piece-goods from Japan fell from 360,000 francs in 1929 to 56,000 francs in 1931.

In *Algeria,* a French colony which enjoys complete Customs Union with France, the *total* Japanese import fell from 4·2 million francs in 1930 to 1·5 millions in 1931.

This was a decline of 67 per cent., or more than three times greater than the fall in value of the import from France in the same period.

No separate statistics for the Japanese piece-goods import exist, but plainly there was a heavy fall.

XV

THE AFRICAN TREATIES

Two international agreements establish a Free Trade system over a vast area of Central Africa. These agreements are relics of the discarded Free Trade system, and constitute one of the obstacles to the achievement of the Customs Union of Britain with the Crown colonies.

The Congo Basin Treaty, also known as the Convention of St. Germain-en-Laye, establishes Free Trade over an area stretching from the West Coast of Africa to the East.

It is a remarkable document. Not only does it include the whole of the Belgian Congo and of our East African colonies of Kenya and Nyasaland, but it also takes in slices of other territories: a corner of Portuguese East Africa, and fragments of Italian Somaliland, Abyssinia, and the Anglo-Egyptian Sudan.

A grave aspect of this treaty situation is that where a portion of a British colony is included in the treaty area, the whole colony must necessarily, for administrative reasons, be precluded from giving preference to Empire countries.

The West African Treaties, or the Anglo-French Convention, establishes Free Trade conditions as between two small French colonies in West Africa, the Ivory Coast and Dahomey, and the important British colonies of Nigeria and the Gold Coast.

We give to the French the same commercial opportunities in Nigeria and the Gold Coast as we ourselves enjoy, in return for a similar right in the French colonies.

But owing to the existence of " most-favoured-

nation '' clauses in numerous commercial treaties
with foreign countries, we must give these countries
the same right of free access to Nigeria and the
Gold Coast as we give to the French.

In the case of the Japanese Commercial Treaty,
the '' most-favoured-nation '' clause has been de-
nounced, and fell into abeyance on May 16th, 1934.

The import of foreign merchandise into these
British colonies is four times as great as the value
of British exports to the French West African
colonies concerned.

XVI

BRITAIN'S TRADE AGREEMENTS WITH FOREIGN COUNTRIES

PACTS THAT OPERATE TO THE ADVANTAGE OF FOREIGNERS

The British Government has made a series of commercial treaties with foreign countries. The chief of these are the agreements with Norway, Sweden, Denmark, Finland, Germany, and the Argentine.

The avowed object of these agreements is stated in the preamble to each, which, in the case of the Argentine agreement, reads: "To increase and facilitate trade and commerce between the Argentine Republic on the one hand and the United Kingdom of Great Britain and Northern Ireland on the other."

To what extent has this object been realized in practice?

The trade returns issued by the Board of Trade for the first quarter of 1934 gave figures for British trade with these six countries. They related to a total trade of £48 millions.

They showed that Britain had gained an additional trade of £1,212,000 with the six "pact countries" as compared with the first quarter of 1933.

They showed that, on the other hand, the six foreign countries had increased their trade with Britain by £3,230,000.

In detail, the results were:

86

1934, 1st quarter.

			Imports into Great Britain.	Exports from Great Britain.
			£	£
Germany	.	.	plus 1,115,000	plus 750,000
Finland	.	.	plus 755,000	plus 145,000
Argentina	.	.	plus 649,000	minus 177,000
Sweden	.	.	plus 776,000	plus 197,000
Norway	.	.	plus 78,000	plus 276,000
Denmark	.	.	minus 143,000	plus 21,000
Net increase	.	.	£3,230,000	£1,212,000

TRADE WITH GERMANY

The German figures proved to be especially interesting. The total British net increase in exports to Germany of £756,000 was more than accounted for by increases in:

	£
Coal and other raw materials . .	628,000
Semi-raw materials (such as cotton yarn, non-ferrous ingots, etc.) . .	166,000
Total .	£794,000

Actually, then, there was a decline in our exports to Germany of manufactured goods.

But the increase in our purchases from Germany are almost entirely an increase in manufactured goods in competition with our own industries.

Some contrasts in specific items were:

Change in first quarter, 1934, compared with first quarter, 1933.

			German exports to Great Britain.	British exports to Germany.
			£	£
Iron and steel manufactures	.		plus 181,000	plus 1,000
Cutlery	.	.	plus 123,000	minus 4,000
Machinery	.	.	plus 100,000	plus 20,000
Clothes	.	.	plus 43,000	minus 4,000
Chemicals	.	.	plus 250,000	plus 2,000
Vehicles	.	.	plus 34,000	minus 134,000
Miscellaneous manufactures	.		plus 71,000	plus 38,000

87

The effect on the trade between Britain and Sweden is revealed by the following table, Sweden enjoying a preponderating advantage in important classes of manufactures:

	Swedish exports to Great Britain. Increases. £	British imports to Sweden. Increases. £
Pottery . . .	16,000	3,000
Iron and steel . .	116,000	24,000
Cutlery . . .	13,000	2,000
Machinery . .	63,000	44,000

THE EMPIRE BUYS MORE

The failure of the British Government's plan to stimulate the export of manufactures by means of trade agreements with foreign countries was revealed in striking fashion by the Board of Trade Returns for the first quarter of 1934.

These figures showed that the whole of the increase in exports of British manufactures as compared with the same quarter of the previous year was due to increased purchases by Empire countries:

	Empire countries. Increase. £	Foreign countries. Decrease. £
Vehicles (including aircraft and locomotive)	1,928,246	2,103,981
Iron and steel goods .	858,336	290,654
Motor-cars . . .	338,105	212,727
Electrical goods . .	459,000	235,000
Machinery . . .	710,000	22,000
Miscellaneous . .	400,000	92,000
Art. silk, linen, etc. .	368,560	5,000
Cutlery . . .	167,000	51,000
Clothes	136,000	52,000
Pottery . . .	92,000	65,722
Plate and sheet glass .	34,950	26,721
Wood manufactures .	34,000	17,000
Manufactured fuel . .	12,294	17,993
Total . .	£5,538,491	£3,191,798

So the net increase in British exports in these important sections—£2,346,693 in one quarter—was accounted for entirely by greater buying by Empire countries. And these are not paltry items of trade. They are main categories of exports responsible for an export trade of £48 millions, or two-thirds of Britain's exports of manufactured goods.

In the remaining categories of exported manufactures, British countries held their own proportionately with foreign countries.

In the export of electrical goods the position as between Empire and foreign markets showed a radical change. Purchases by Empire countries rose from £558,000 in the first three months of 1933 to £1,017,000 in the first three months of 1934. Foreign purchases fell from £1,044,000 to £809,000.

XVII

THE FRENCH COLONIES

The colonial possessions of France are found principally in Africa, where they extend from the Mediterranean to the Congo, and in Indo-China. The population is about 62 millions, a figure somewhat larger than that of the British Crown colonies, and the area about 5 million square miles, as compared with the 3 million square miles of the British colonial possessions. It must be borne in mind, however, that the French colonies include vast tracts of the Sahara Desert.

Of the population, 20 millions are in the Asiatic possessions of Indo-China and French India, the great part of the remainder being in the African colonies.

There are, in addition, 7 millions in the mandated territories of Syria, Cameroons, and Togoland.

France has made considerable advance towards a Customs Union between herself and her colonies. In the case of Algeria, the Customs Union is complete, and the colony is regarded as an integral part of France.

In the case of the other French colonies, Tunisia, French Indo-China, etc., the Customs Union structure is still being built, but a strong movement exists which, year by year, breaks down the tariff barriers between France and the colonies, and builds up higher barriers between these colonies and foreign countries.

The results of this persistent and energetic drive are shown in the French trade statistics.

France's trade with her colonies grew fourfold

between 1913 and 1926. She has now over 50 per cent. of the total trade of the French colonies.

In the case of Algeria, which is in a state of Empire Free Trade with France, economic relations are exceptionally close. France has 67 per cent. of the total trade of Algeria, and 76 per cent. of the total imports of the colony come from France. Similarly, 60 per cent. of the goods imported into Tunis are from France.

The importance of the colonial trade in the economic life of France is shown by the fact that about 20 per cent. of France's total exports in 1930 were exports to French colonies. Last year, 10 per cent. of Britain's total export trade went to the British Crown colonies.

The vigorous nature of France's colonial policy in recent years is demonstrated by the fact that since 1928 the French Government have lent £60 millions to the colonies for purposes of development.

The British Government, generous in its loans to foreign countries and to mandated territories like Palestine, has lent only about £3 millions to British Crown colonies in the same period.

The French colonies are each directly represented in the French Parliament, a factor which has contributed greatly to the unification of the economic structure.

XVIII

COLONIES OF THE UNITED STATES

The colonial possessions of the United States (Hawaii, the Philippine Islands, Guam, American Samoa, Porto Rico, and the Panama Canal Zone) have a population of 13,700,000, of whom 12 millions are in the Philippine Islands.

These colonies enjoy the benefits of Customs Union with the United States and, as a result, the greater part of their trade is with the mother country.

In the case of the imports of the colonies, the United States has about 78 per cent. of the total trade. The advantages of the union are seen in the remarkable economic development of the colonies. The facts relating to Porto Rico are given on p. 94.

In the case of Hawaii, a comparison with the British island colony of Fiji, also in the Pacific, and with a somewhat larger area than Hawaii, shows that the population of Hawaii, which was smaller than that of Fiji thirty-five years ago, is now twice as large.

In the same way, the imports of Hawaii are twelve times those of Fiji, while her exports are thirteen times greater.

It should be pointed out, however, that Hawaii, unlike Fiji, has an important naval base, and has also better sea communications than Fiji.

XIX

THE JAPANESE POSSESSIONS

The colonial possessions of Japan are found on the eastern mainland of Asia and off the Asiatic coast. They consist of Korea, Formosa, Saghalin, the Kwantung Peninsula, and various islands in the Pacific Ocean.

Total area, 110,685 square miles. Population, 25,863,000.

The most important of the Japanese possessions, Korea, Formosa, and Saghalin, are in complete Customs Union with Japan.

In 1931, the total imports of Korea were £27 millions (at par), of which £22 millions (80 per cent.) came from Japan. The exports were £26 millions, of which £23½ millions (90 per cent.) went to Japan.

In the case of Formosa, the total imports in 1931 were £14½ millions, of which £11½ millions (80 per cent.) came from Japan. The exports were £22 millions, of which £20 millions (91 per cent.) went to Japan.

Manchukuo, formerly a province of China, is now in the power of Japan. Its area is 460,000 square miles, its population 34 millions. It will be rapidly incorporated in the Japanese Customs Union.

XX

WHAT EMPIRE FREE TRADE CAN DO

The Contrast of Jamaica and Porto Rico

Porto Rico is an American island possession in the Caribbean Sea.

Jamaica is a British Crown colony in the same sea, 550 miles away.

The two islands are remarkably similar. But there is one great difference between them: Porto Rico is in full Customs Union with the United States. Jamaica is not in Customs Union with Great Britain.

A quarter of a century ago, Porto Rico and Jamaica, with approximately the same area and a population of about a million, carried on with other countries the same amount of import and export trade.

Of these two islands, Jamaica has greater natural wealth and bigger possibilities for development.

Porto Rico's total trade has increased by 500 per cent. over the last twenty-five years. Jamaica's in the same period has not even doubled itself.

In 1932, Porto Rico's total trade amounted to £19 a head. Jamaica's was only £6 a head—a third of Porto Rico's.

Of the total imports of Porto Rico in that year (£12,250,000 at par), no less than £10,560,000 were bought from the United States. That is 86 per cent. of the total.

Jamaica's imports were £4,754,000, of which £1,890,000 came from Great Britain—39 per cent. Porto Rico spent £7 a head in the United States. Jamaica spent £1 16s. a head in Britain.

But in this there was no disadvantage to the American colony. Porto Rico had a favourable trade balance. Jamaica's was unfavourable.

Porto Rico's exports were £17 millions, of which 95 per cent. went to the United States. Jamaica's exports were £3 millions, of which about 50 per cent. went to Great Britain.

XXI

AGRICULTURAL PRODUCTION IN ENGLAND AND WALES

Since the National Government came into office, two harvests have been brought in. Another will soon be reaped.

In that time there has been no increase in the production of the farms of Britain. It is true that there have been increases in such crops as wheat, which is assisted by a subsidy, potatoes, mangolds, and sugar-beet.

But these have been offset by decreases in the production of oats, barley, and other crops.

Taking livestock as a whole, there is no increase in production.

The estimated gross value of the agricultural output in the cereal year 1931–2 was only £183,670,000, as compared with £235,060,000 in 1925.

Imports of Foodstuffs since Ottawa

In the year 1933, eighteen months after the Ottawa agreements, Great Britain was still purchasing from foreign countries £167,136,000 of foodstuffs.

From the Empire, Britain was taking £119,757,000 of food.

In other words, Britain was spending £47 millions more with the foreigners than with the producers in her own Empire.

In the first four months of 1934, the purchases of food from foreign countries were £56,262,000, from Empire countries, £45,267,000.

Note.—These figures are taken from incomplete records, but it can be assumed that the totals are approximately correct.

XXII

IMPORTS OF FOODSTUFFS FROM THE UNITED STATES

In the years from 1919 to 1934 (first four months), Britain spent £1,141,016,000 on foodstuffs imported from the United States.

This sum is considerably larger than the amount of the British War Debt to the United States, which was funded at $4,600 millions, or approximately £910 millions at par.

XXIII

MANY TONGUES, ONE MIND

In Russia there are, according to the compilations of the authorities, 169 races and about 150 languages.

No estimate exists, so far as I can ascertain, of the number of races and languages in the British Empire. No doubt there are many, particularly in the Indian Empire, where 220 languages are spoken.

But the Russian statistics show that a multiplicity of languages and races can be knitted together in a common bond of unity under one central Government, to which is delegated authority and power.

XXIV

THE GLORY OF IT

Empire Free Trade is like a great and gracious figure walking through the capitals of the Empire, leading two children by the hand. The two children are called Isolation and High Wages.

These are two policies subsidiary to the main policy of Empire Free Trade, but springing from it, as naturally and inevitably as the branches of a tree from the trunk.

Empire Free Trade means the consolidation of the Empire. It means that we are bent on creating a united commonwealth so powerful that it will enable us to detach ourselves from dangerous and delusive associations with foreign countries.

Splendid Isolation is derided by the politicians. But that is always the way. A bold determined policy, involving a break with methods of compromise, is accepted with difficulty by unimaginative and timid men.

But Splendid Isolation has been the traditional policy of the Conservative Party through the ages. It is true that there have been departures from it from time to time. But these departures never boded well for the peace and welfare of Britain.

In any case, we are not concerned with the past. Our eyes must be turned to the future. We must resolve not to take part in any European war.

We must send no more expeditionary forces to the Continent under any pretext. Here let us stand in our stronghold, with our navy, our army, and our air force strong enough to protect the preserves and the highways of the Empire. We court no friend and we fear no enemy.

In this policy we should stand in the closest relations of friendship with the United States, the watch-tower of the Western world, united to us by the bonds of common race and language.

As for High Wages, all the manufacturing countries of the Empire are high-wage countries. But we must not be content with the prevailing standards. There is no use shutting our eyes to the fact that a new cycle of prosperity for Britain must be based upon rates of pay higher than at present. We must be prepared to raise wages and salaries. If you do not accept this, you are out of touch with the spirit animating the policy of Empire.

We must increase the purchasing power of the Crown colonies. That is a task laid upon us. We must perform it, not only in justice to them, but in order to reap the reward of their increased ability to buy. We want to bring the harvest home to our own barns, for in the increased purchasing power of the Crown colonies lies the hope of the manufacturing population of Lancashire.

For nearly a quarter of a century I have pleaded this cause. Looking back over the years, I am surprised at the opposition faced by Joseph Chamberlain, who gave us the land on which we are endeavouring to build the house.

Bonar Law was fully alive to all the possibilities, and intended—had he lived—to give the touch of political reality to the ideal which had been handed on to his keeping.

I had been the remote but devoted follower of Joseph Chamberlain, putting my political fortunes to the test on his behalf. It was never my good fortune to hear him speak. I once saw him in his last years in a foreign land.

It was as the servant of Bonar Law, but in intimate relationship carrying out the daily tasks and duties, that I hoped to contribute some definite measures of help to the policy which meant so much to Britain and the dominions.

But when death took him, and the body of this first Prime Minister from the dominions was laid to rest in Westminster Abbey, there seemed no leader to take his place. For a time, the Empire spirit was hushed to sleep.

I was conscious that I did not possess the personal qualities which leadership demanded of a man.

But a time came when the search for someone willing to take up the burden grew wearisome. Precious, vital years were passing without progress, and I was compelled to examine my conscience. Believing as I did in the policy, I would not escape responsibility because of my awareness of personal unworthiness.

I assumed reluctantly the task of launching and carrying on a new campaign for the old cause. In the course of the persistent agitation that has been carried on since, so full of trials and disappointments as well as triumphs and exultations, I have made many new comrades of sterling worth.

But I have done more. I have found qualities in myself which were not there before. The greatness of the work has been an inspiring and elevating influence.

It was a case of the man borrowing his stature from the task.

It is plain to all that we will reach our goal earlier or later. If a leader arises to carry our banner, we are sure to make rapid progress. It is a pity indeed that we have not now got a Joseph Chamberlain or a Bonar Law to lift the banner up, to adorn it and beautify it, so that men might accept it in all its glory.

We must be patient. We must endure without complaint, vigilant and resolute in the pursuit of our adventure. And in humility, we join in the plea—

" And now, O God, what wait we for? Our hope is in Thee."

THE COMMODITIES OF THE EMPIRE

Commodity.				Empire production. Million qrs.	Percentage of world total.
Wheat	.	.	.	129	20
Oats	.	.	.	61	13
Barley	.	.	.	28	12

The Empire produces more wheat than it consumes, yet Britain imports wheat from the Argentine and other foreign countries. In the case of oats and barley, there is a small Empire deficiency which can be made up as soon as the resolution is taken to do so.

Commodity.				Empire production. Tons.	Percentage of world total.
Cocoa	.	.	.	260,000	47
Cattle	.	.	.	214,499,000	39
Sheep	.	.	.	226,708,000	36

In spite of these immense Empire herds and flocks Britain, owning in her dominions and dependencies nearly four out of every ten head of cattle in the world, imports beef from the Argentine and elsewhere. There is a great opportunity for developing an Empire beef-raising industry, especially in the rich pasture-lands of Southern Rhodesia.

Commodity.				Empire production. Tons.	Percentage of world total.
Cotton	.	.	.	1,000,000	20
Wool	.	.	.	700,000	42
Jute	.	.	.	1,050,000	98

There are great opportunities for the development of cotton growing in the Empire, especially in the Sudan and in Kenya, under a well-organized scheme of production.

Commodity.	Empire production.	Percentage of world total.
Silver . . .	31,350,000 oz.	19
Gold . . .	15,000,000 oz.	62
Tin	33,337 tons	37
Lead	300,000 tons	30
Nickel . . .	17,000 tons	68
Manganese . .	882,000 tons	33
Copper (restricted) .	95,000 tons	$9\frac{1}{2}$
Platinum . . .	81,000 oz.	29

Although the present Empire production of copper is small and not adequate to its needs, the resources of copper ore that are waiting to be exploited in the Empire, and above all in Northern Rhodesia, are of immense value. The Empire is destined to be self-supporting in this metal.

Commodity.	Empire production. Tons.	Percentage of world total.
Rubber . . .	500,000	70
Asbestos . . .	321,000	90
Coal	210,000,000	22

In addition to this production of bituminous coal there are great deposits of anthracite coal in Britain. These are half as big as the reserves in the United States, yet the production of this coal in America is more than ten times our production here.

In the case of timber, the Empire has a forest area of 2,300,000 square miles, but less than a third of it is at present in commercial use. There is no reason why, with proper organization of production, the Empire should not be self-supporting in timber.

Commodity.	Empire production. Gallons.	Percentage of world total.
Petroleum . . .	700,000,000	$1\frac{1}{2}$

Trinidad is the chief source of supplies, but other oil-fields in the Empire will be uncovered, and there is no reason to despair of a large increase in Empire production.

APPENDIX II

POINTS FOR SPEAKERS

The foreigner is stealing the British egg market.

The foreigner is ruining the British egg producer.

In the first three months of 1934 the foreigner sent us practically as many eggs as he sent in the same months of 1933.

The Empire import was reduced by a quarter.

Why were the imports from the foreigners not reduced by a quarter also?

Because the Government is good to the Danes and the Dutch.

Rhodesia's Prime Minister said in the Rhodesian Parliament that Britain has one last chance of establishing Empire Free Trade with Rhodesia.

Why does he complain?

Because although Rhodesia buys more from Britain than she sells to Britain, yet Rhodesian maize is excluded from Britain for the benefit of the Argentine.

But the Argentine sells four times as much to Britain as she buys from Britain.

Who is helping the foreigner at the expense of the British Empire?

Rhodesia sells to Britain tobacco, maize, oranges, and asbestos.

None of these competes with British producers.

Rhodesia wants Empire Free Trade.

The Argentine sells us beef.

The beef competes with British producers.

The Argentine does not want Empire Free Trade.

Why is it that the Argentine gets the ear of the British Government while Rhodesia is turned coldly away?

It would be a lie to say that—

New Zealand is damaging the British dairy farmer.

Last year New Zealand sent us only 2½ million cwts. of butter, while foreign countries sent 3½ million cwts.

There is room in the market for both the British farmer and the New Zealand producer, if we shut out the foreigner.

New Zealand offers us Empire Free Trade.

The British Government has rejected it.

It would be a lie to say that—

The British dairy farmer is threatened with ruin because of butter imports from Australia.

Last year, Australia sent us 100,000 cwts. of butter *less* than the year before.

But Russia sent 240,000 cwts. *more.*

Holland sent 100,000 cwts. *more.*

It would be a lie to say that—

The British dairy farmer is menaced by imports from the dominions.

In the first three months of 1934 our import of condensed milk from British countries *fell* by £37,000 when compared with the same period of 1933.

But our import from foreign countries *increased* by £38,000.

We took that sum of money from the British producers overseas and gave it to the foreigners.

It would be a lie to say that—

The British dominions are the enemies of the British dairy farmer.

It is the foreign producers who are the enemies of the dairy farmer.

In the six months September 1933 to February 1934, our imports of butter from British countries increased by 69,000 cwts. over the same period in the previous year.

But our imports from foreign countries rose by 169,000 cwts.

The British Government has in effect been offered Empire Free Trade by New Zealand, and could avail itself of that offer by diverting orders for butter from foreign countries to producers in Britain and the dominions.

It would be a lie to say that—

The British dominions damage our pig producers.

It would be true to say that we are buying more chilled and frozen pork—but we are buying a bigger proportion of it from foreign lands.

In the first three months of 1934 we took 70,000 cwts. more of this pork from British countries than in the same months of 1933. But we bought 103,000 cwts. *more* of it from foreigners.

Do you know that Mr. Runciman's Ministry, the Board of Trade, makes a grant to the Danish and other foreign bacon producers of £1 million a month?

These foreigners are sending us less bacon. But we are paying them more for it.

The extra cost is a million a month just now. It is 65 per cent. more than we used to pay.

There is no reason why we should pay this sum. We could keep the Danish bacon imports down by imposing duties. The Danes would have to pay those duties.

But Mr. Runciman imposes quotas. He makes *us* pay the money.

To the City Financiers

"Where your treasure is, there will your heart be also."

The money-changers say, if we do not buy from the British dominions to whom we have lent money, we will not get our interest.

Australia owes this country £596 millions.

New Zealand owes us £172 millions.

A total of £768 millions.

But the Argentine owes Britain only £500 millions.

Your treasure is in the Empire. Your heart should be there also.

We bought £47,000 more tin ore from British countries during the first three months of 1934 than during the same period in the previous year.

It is an increase of 25 per cent.

But our purchases of tin ore from foreign countries rose by £334,000, *or* 100 *per cent.*!

We buy from Bolivia and Chile, which spend only a shilling or two in this country for every pound we spend in their markets.

We ought to take our tin from Nigeria and other Empire countries that want to deal with us.

In the first three months of 1934 we bought 70,000 cubic feet of railway sleepers from British countries. That was 80,000 less than in the same months of the year before.

But we took a million cubic feet from the foreigners, an *increase* of 517,000 cubic feet.

Why should we buy these sleepers from the Russians and the Poles? What madness is this?

We ought to be buying from the Empire, not from these foreign countries.

We are eating less British salmon and more foreign salmon.

In the first three months of 1934 we spent £42,000 less than in the same period in 1933 in purchases of salmon from British countries.

But we spent £90,000 more in salmon from foreigners.

Canada lost business in this market amounting to £40,000. The Russians *gained* £50,000 worth.

It is monstrous that we should transfer these orders from the Canadians to the Russians.

Canada spends £21 millions a year in Britain. Russia spends £3 millions.

During the first three months of 1934 Britain bought from foreign countries £433,000 more of tinned and bottled fruit than in the same period in 1933.

But our purchases from British countries increased by only £35,000.

We buy our tinned fruit from the Americans, paying them at the rate of £3½ millions a year for it.

Why should we send all that money to the Americans, who do not buy from us, when we can get our fruit from Malaya and Australia and the West Indies?

Our imports of coffee from British countries are down by £320,000 in the first three months of 1934 as compared with the same period in 1933.

But our imports from foreign countries *rose* by £56,000.

We take British-grown coffee from Kenya and foreign coffee from Costa Rica.

Kenya buys from us more than we buy from her. Costa Rica buys from us a negligible amount.

Let us buy our coffee from the British countries which spend their money here.

If you spend a shilling on Australian butter, *every penny* of that shilling comes back to this country in the form of purchases by the Australians of British goods or interest-payments on British money invested in Australia.

If you spend a shilling on Danish butter, only 3¾*d.* out of your shilling will be spent by the Danes in this country.

If you spend a shilling on Russian butter, only 2*d.* of the shilling comes back to Britain to give work to our people.

Buy your butter from the Empire countries which buy from us. Shun the butter from foreigners, who do not spend their money in Britain.

INDEX